AF884358

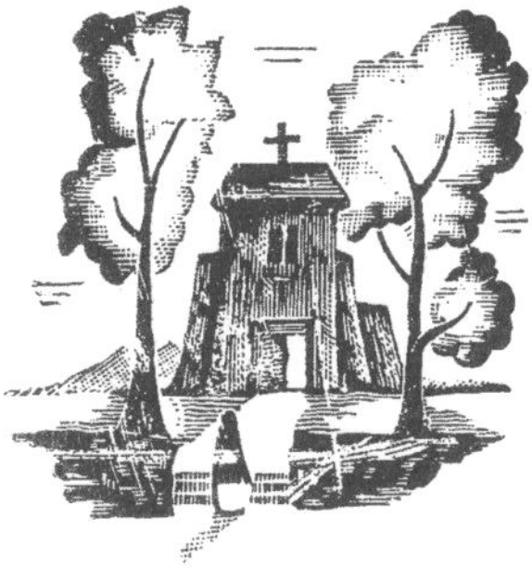

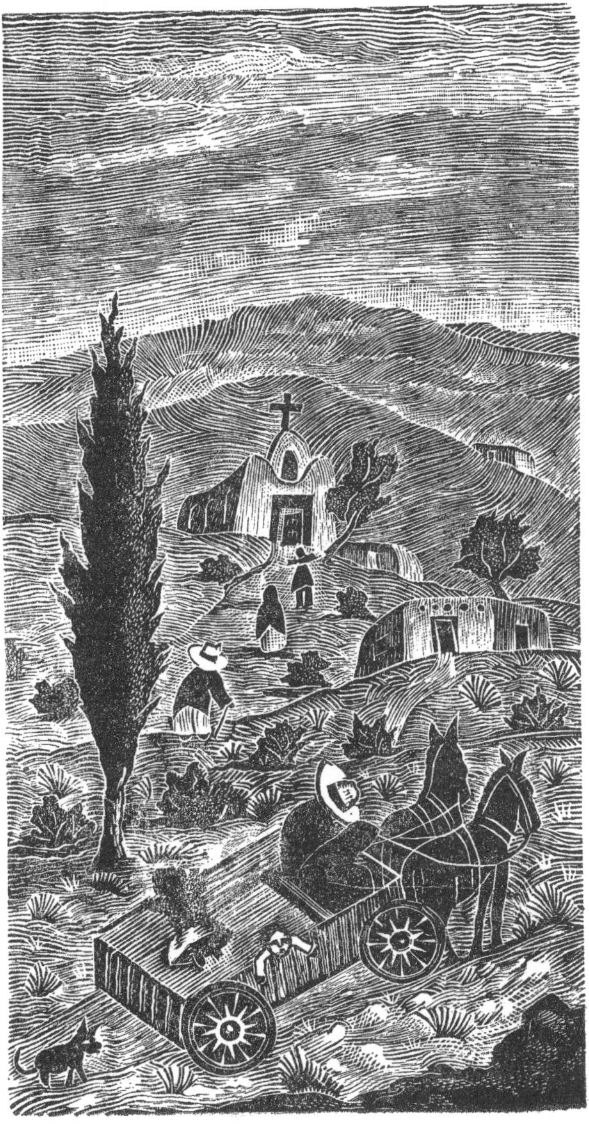

REMEMBERING SANTA FE

Written & Illustrated by

Willard F. Clark

Gibbs Smith, Publisher
Salt Lake City

08 07 06 05 04 5 4 3 2 1

Copyright © 1990 Willard Clark

Copyright © 2004 Kevin Ryan

All rights reserved. No part of this book may be reproduced by any means whatsoever without written permission from the publisher, except brief portions quoted for purpose of review.

Published by

Gibbs Smith, Publisher

P.O. Box 667

Layton, Utah 84041

Orders: (1-800) 748-5439

www.gibbs-smith.com

Printed and bound in Hong Kong

First printed as a limited edition in 1990 by Clark's Studio
First printed as a trade edition in 1990 by Blue Feather Press
Reprinted in 2004 by Gibbs Smith, Publisher

LIBRARY OF CONGRESS CATALOGING-IN-PUBLICATION DATA

Clark, Willard F., 1910-1992.
[Recuerdos de Santa Fe, 1928-1943]
Remembering Santa Fe / written and illustrated by Willard F. Clark ; foreword by Kevin Ryan.
p. cm.
Originally published: Recuerdos de Santa Fe, 1928-1943. Santa Fe : Clark's Studio, 1990.
ISBN 1-58685-359-7
1. Clark, Willard F., 1910-1992. 2. Santa Fe (N.M.)—In art. 3. Santa Fe (N.M.)—Description and travel. I. Title.

NE1300.6.C58A4 2004
769.92—dc22

2003063313

FOREWORD

My grandfather, Willard F. Clark, was born in a suburb of Boston in 1910. Soon his family moved to Argentina, where his father was in the import-export business and later was president of General Motors for Argentina. As a teenager, Willard spent his summers in New York City, studying art at Grand Central Station Art School and the Hawthorn Art Academy. In New York, he also spent time with an uncle who was a carpenter foreman for ship builders. His uncle had models of clipper ships in bottles in the Smithsonian. Grandpa later told me that these ships are what first interested him in becoming a craftsman.

In 1928 on his way to California, Willard stopped in Santa Fe and quickly fell in love with the town. He said it reminded him of a village in the foothills of the Andes. It helped that he was fluent in Spanish, as Santa Fe and northern New Mexico were mostly Spanish-speaking areas. Willard decided to stay.

He needed to find a way to make a living in a small town of seven thousand. He saw that there was no full-service print shop and realized this was something he could do. In addition he could add his artwork to the jobs, something only a few others in the entire country were doing. He started a small print shop in Sena Plaza, teaching himself the craft of printing—getting zinc plates made, cutting his own woodblocks, setting type, and binding small books. He also did other things while working to build up his printing business. He painted decorative scenes of the people and places of northern New Mexico on fireplace chimneys, around doorways, and on furniture such as headboards and dressers. He even painted a few murals in bars. He started to develop a graphic style that came to represent, to many around the world, Santa Fe and northern New Mexico.

In 1930 Willard married my grandmother, Bertha Berchtold, whose family had arrived in New Mexico in 1912. He decided to build a two-story adobe house; he would have his print shop downstairs and his living quarters upstairs. Soon he had not only a wife but two daughters. Over the next twelve years he built up the business until it was very busy. He had a lot of equipment, two full-time employees, and plenty of work. My grandma did the accounting, secretarial, and delivery work for the shop. The evenings were the only time Grandpa had to produce his artwork and woodcuts. Many times he would create art at night that was needed to print the next day. He did printing for many of the businesses of Santa Fe, including announcements; programs for events; tourist literature of all sorts; brochures for hotels in Santa Fe, Albuquerque, and Taos; menus; letterheads; advertisements; "Do Not Disturb" signs for La Fonda Hotel; brochures; and catalogs. During this time he got to know many of the local artists, including Gerald Cassidy, Josef Bakos, Fremont Ellis, Oliver Rush, and especially Will Shuster and Gustave Baumann, with whom he became good friends. He printed a variety of projects for Baumann, including his book *Frijoles Canyon Pictographs.*

In 1943 Willard decided to close up the print shop and go to work in Los Alamos as a machinist for the Manhattan Project. His plan was to return after the war, but he ended up staying until his retirement in 1973. During this time he continued to be very creative; he did portrait and landscape painting, wood carving, cement sculpture, and made jewelry. In 1965 he and my mother opened a gallery on Canyon Road, where they sold imports from around the world along with his paintings and jewelry. In 1974 I went to work for a year in the gallery. There I learned to make jewelry, woodcarvings, and watercolors. On Sundays we would go to his studio to do the last wax castings for jewelry in silver and gold. This was when I got to see all of his woodblocks, commercial art, and fine art prints. I could not believe the amount of creative work that existed, in addition to what he was then producing.

I moved across the street from Grandpa in 1983. In 1985 he renewed his interest in printing. He became good friends with Pam Smith, who owned a small print shop and ran the Palace of Governor's Museum Press. With her encouragement, he bought a 1910 Potter Proof Press, got out his old engraving and woodcutting tools to make new prints, and dusted off the old woodblocks from the 1930s and '40s. He made up a portfolio of 180 prints to show to an ever-increasing number of interested collectors. My Saturday afternoons were often spent with him showing me about the printing process.

In 1988 Willard decided to make a book about his memories of Santa Fe, including nearby villages and landmarks. Because of his many other projects, it took him two years to complete the forty-six wood engravings, the four-color frontispiece, and the large woodcut for the cover. During that time he also wrote the text and had the type set for the book. Then, for each engraving, he rolled the hand-ground ink on the woodblock, put the paper on the press, and hand-cranked each page of the 100 limited-edition books. He then signed each print. Each text page needed to go through the press three times, and by 1992 he had completed sixty of the books—including text pages, all of the prints, the covers, and the hand-binding. This was to become *Recuerdos de Santa Fe, 1928–1943*.

Suffering a stroke in June 1992, he was unable to finish the remaining forty books. He asked me if I would complete the printing of the books, learn to print his woodcuts, and do some of my own woodcuts. For the next six months, until his death on December 12, 1992, I worked and studied with him every day. I had always greatly admired my grandfather, but after seeing what he accomplished with this book, as well as all his other work, my admiration for him grew immensely.

Kevin Ryan
Grandson of Willard F. Clark

INTRODUCTION

To My Papa

Santa Fe is a very ancient city. Our family has lived here since 1912. My father arrived in 1928, and has witnessed its evolution into what it is today. He is completely at home here because he was raised in Argentina, where he spoke Spanish as his first language, and the two cultures are so similar. This was especially true before so many Anglos arrived, and the city was mostly populated by the Spanish, Mexicans and the Indians.

Writing this introduction is one of the high points in my life, because this book is such a special gift to all of us who love Santa Fe and its past, and who love and admire my father.

These prints are wonderful, funny and exquisite, from an artistic point of view. Many of the "memories" they depict are my memories, too. They truly portray the essence of Santa Fe during this period (1928-1943).

Doris Clark Senutovitch
Santa Fe, New Mexico

With love to my wife Bertha
and my daughters Doris and Bertha

1

LAMY

1928, the train was the way to go for any distance. When I look back, a great way it was! Lamy was the closest railroad station for Santa Fe—about 20 miles. It also had a very small Fred Harvey Inn and Restaurant which later turned out to be a very pleasant place to go for a little drive and a good dinner.

In getting off the train, the reception committee amounted to a man in a cowboy outfit with a gun on his belt, a couple of railroad workers, and another passenger, a major change from the east.

Sorry to see the railroads go.

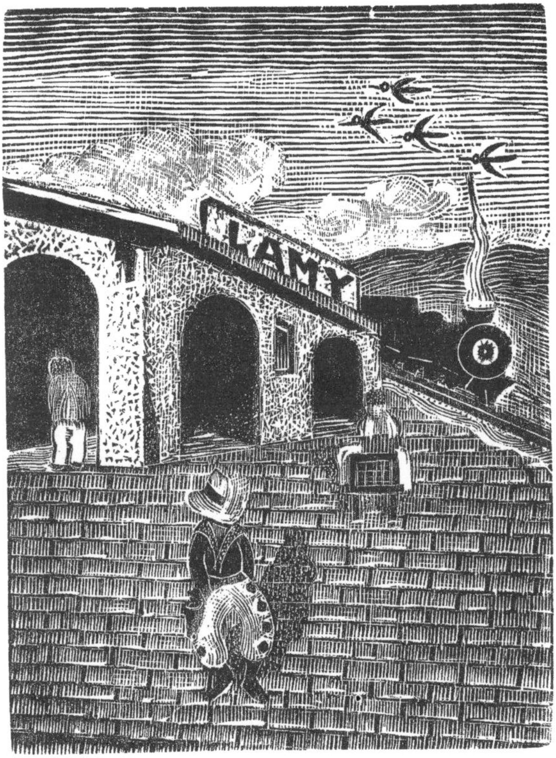
LAMY

2

TO SANTA FE

The cowboy was the driver of the open-top touring car that was our transporation to Santa Fe.

Dirt road, rolling semi-desert country, no fences, rabbits running across the road, beautiful blue sky, piñon-covered hills: reminded me of the country I was raised in—Argentina, South America. Spent some time in the foothills of the Andes.

I was already feeling good about this country and looking forward to seeing Santa Fe.

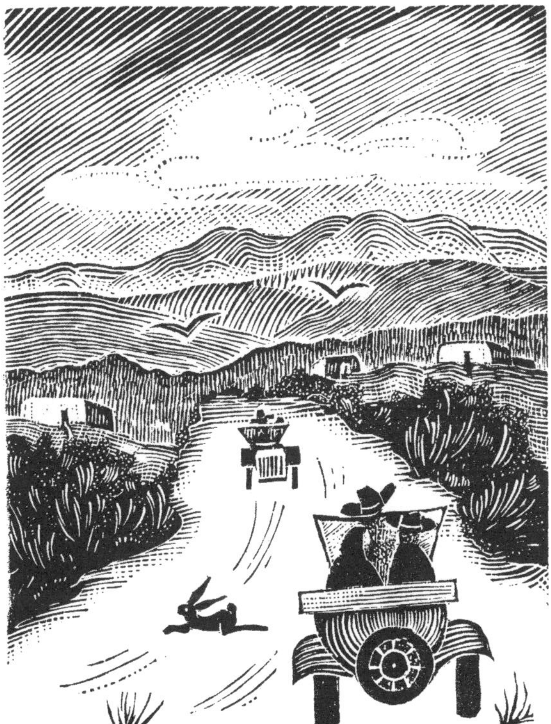

3

SANTA FE

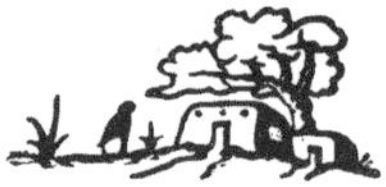

Came in on the Las Vegas highway onto what was then College Street to La Fonda Hotel on the plaza.

The plaza, a basic design used by the Spaniards all over the world, is so functional. If you need to do some shopping it is all right there under the portales of the buildings that surround the park. If you are old, you sit on a bench and hope an old friend will come by and sit with you. If you are young, a stroll through the park may brighten your day with a smile from a pretty girl.

The band concerts on Sunday, the fiestas, the dancing in the park. . . .

Now the old stores and shops are art galleries, boutiques—you never see anyone you know. The tourists have taken over and the plaza no longer belongs to the people of the village.

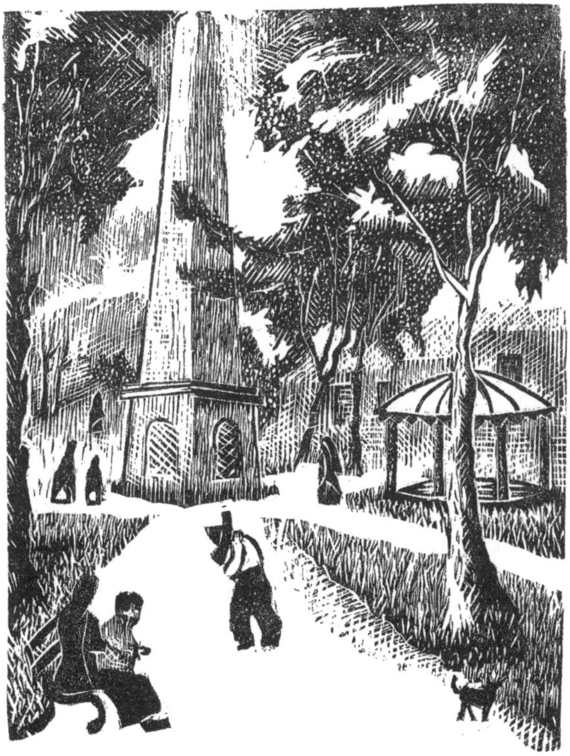

4

LA FONDA HOTEL

Not very long before I came to Santa Fe, the Fred Harvey system had remodeled the very old La Fonda Hotel into a two story building. The furnishings were hand-carved, there was a lot of wrought-iron and local tin work, hand painted bed-headboards, and Navajo and Chimayo rugs.

Fred Harvey was renowned for the service and the quality of the dining room. There were live orchestras and dancing in the evenings.

This hotel is special for me, because they were to be one of my best accounts for the print shop, and I proposed to my wife there and we celebrated just about every anniversary for 51 years at La Fonda Hotel.

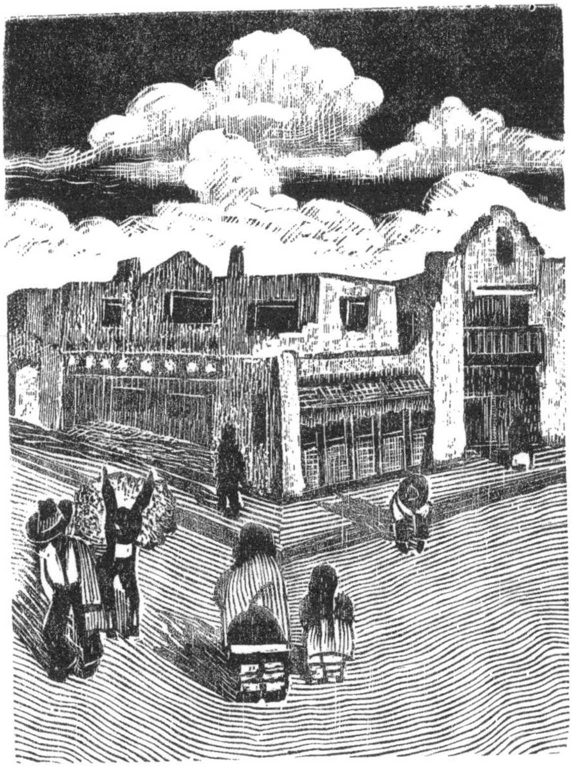

5

THE PALACE OF THE GOVERNORS

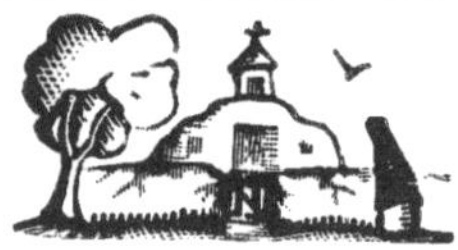

This very old building takes up the whole north side of the plaza, a very important part of our history which cannot be dealt with in this modest "Recuerdos" of mine.

My first impression was of great age as you walk through the rooms, the very thick adobe walls, the very old wood floors, vigas, and carved corbels. You also feel the drama of the centuries that have passed.

The print shop in the courtyard of this museum, managed by Pam Smith with the old letter press, hand set type and hand bindery, is not just a museum display but a working productive print shop turning out beautiful books.

Pam was one of the most persistent people who got me going after being dormant as a printer and wood engraver for over 40 years.

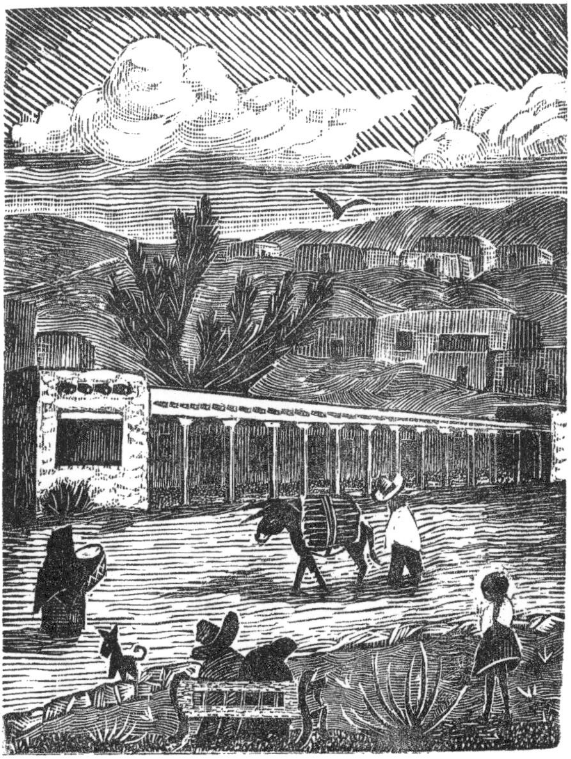

6

GUADALUPE CHURCH

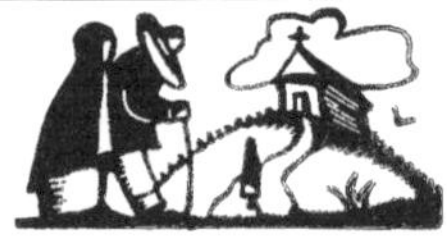

Many old Catholic churches in this area: certainly a very important part of the lives of the Spanish people.

They use their church in their daily living—not just on Sunday. From birth to death they know just what to do; and if they slip up, confession helps to get them going again.

Sorry to say, this church has been remodeled on the inside for exhibits, concerts, etc. Better than shops and galleries.

The very old painting of Guadalupe that was the background for the altar has been restored and, as usual, destroyed.

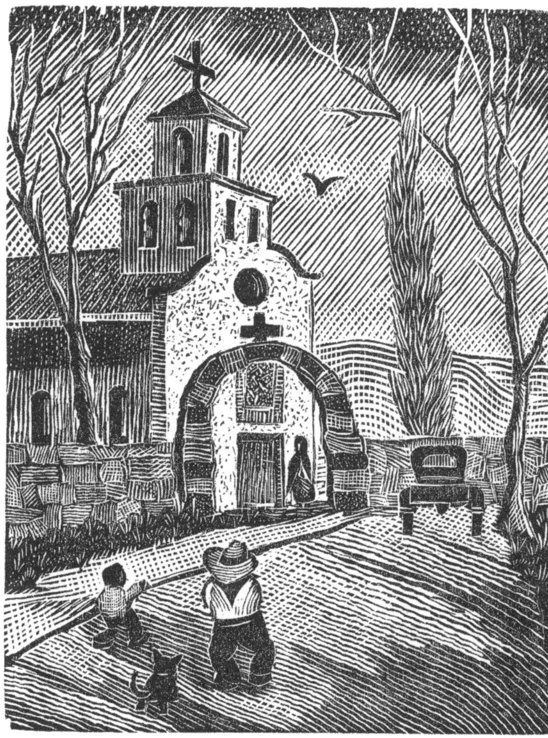

7

THE OLDEST HOUSE

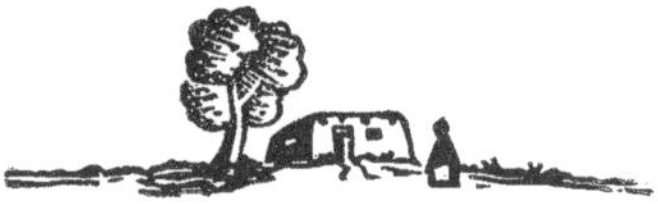

My first visit to this house next to the oldest church was interesting because that is what it was—a very old house with people living in it, with claims that it was the oldest house in the U.S.

This may or may not be true, but old it certainly was, built with very thick walls and probably no foundation.

It seems a shame you cannot protect and leave something that has so much history so our children and grandchildren can also enjoy it as it was. Instead, you make a store out of it, fill it with trinkets and charge admission.

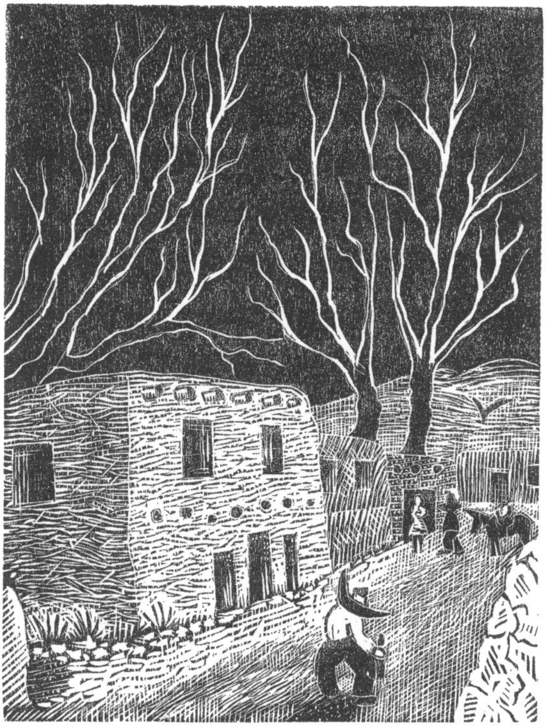

8

ST. FRANCIS CATHEDRAL

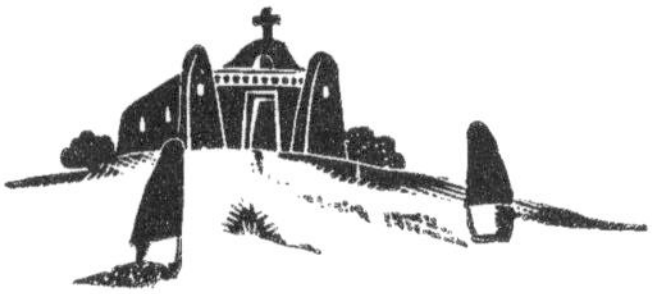

The walls of the Cathedral were built around the old parroquia church about 1880 during the time of Archbishop Lamy by Italian stone masons—a definite contrast from the usual adobe of this area.

It is my understanding that the towers were never finished and that the stone came from an area near Lamy.

Like Catholic Spanish towns everywhere, this is the center of the spiritual life of the people and is usually a dominant structure. Now it is getting some competition from a parking garage.

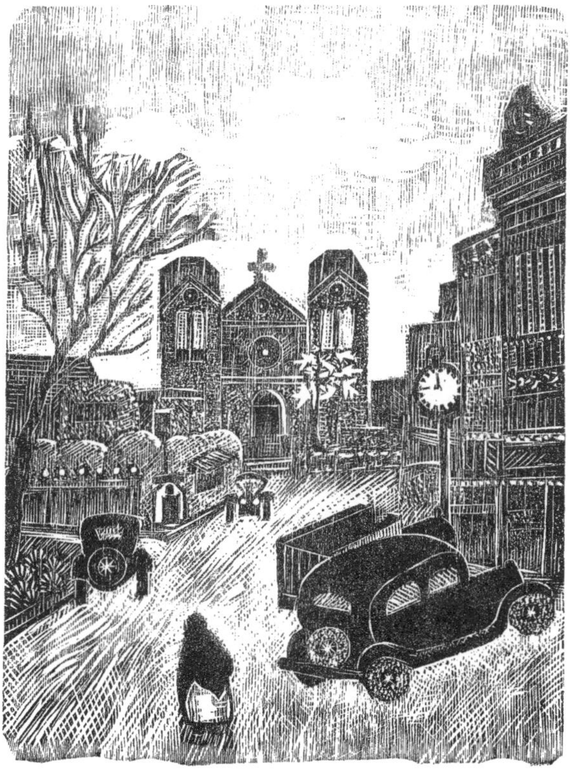

9

CANYON ROAD AND CAMINO DEL MONTE SOL

Most all of the streets were dirt, which was a part of the character of the town.

Camino del Monte Sol became known as the road the "Cinco Pintores" (the five painters) built their homes and studios on. The painters are now all dead, the road is paved—but it retains some of the old charm.

Canyon Road was practically all homes and the way you went to our only water supply: a couple of small dams to catch the melted snow from the mountains. When there was not much snow, the water was rationed. What great drinking water!

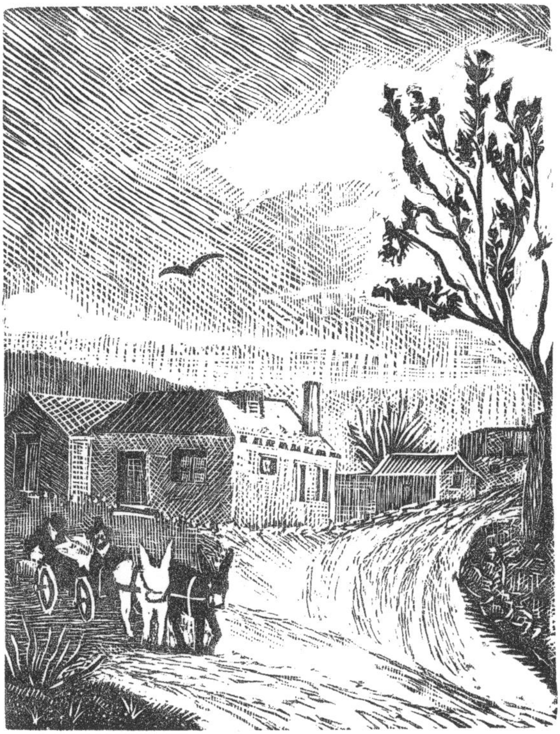

10

THE OLDEST CHURCH

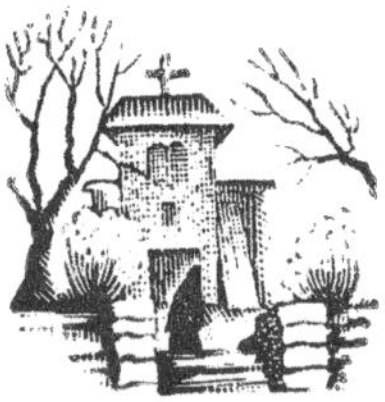

Here is the oldest church as it was on my first visit. It was remodeled a number of times before and again after this print was made.

Services were still being held and there was no charge just to go in and enjoy the very old and beautiful interior. There is much history in this building and it is one of the most important things to see today.

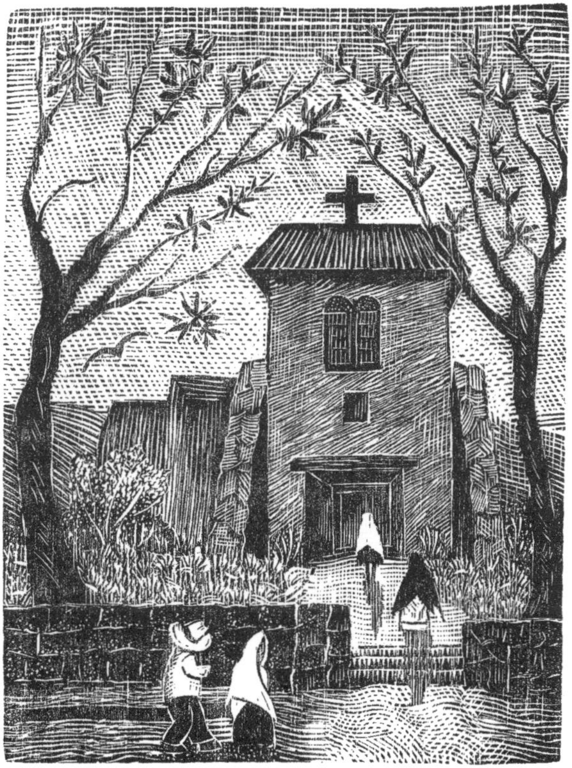

11

MY FIRST RENTED HOUSE

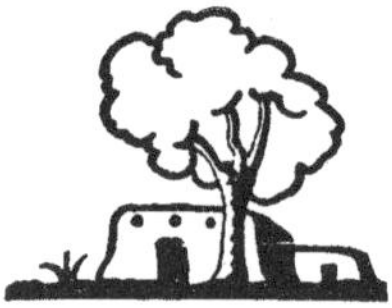

Outside plumbing was not unusual at this time. It was not all bad, could be a social experience, though the winter discourages reading.

Had a bath tub in the kitchen with a folding screen around it. Hot water had to be done on top of the wood and coal Black Beauty kitchen stove, this luxury being reserved for Saturday.

The heat was the usual little corner fireplaces; snuggling and blankets were popular. This memory also was not all that bad.

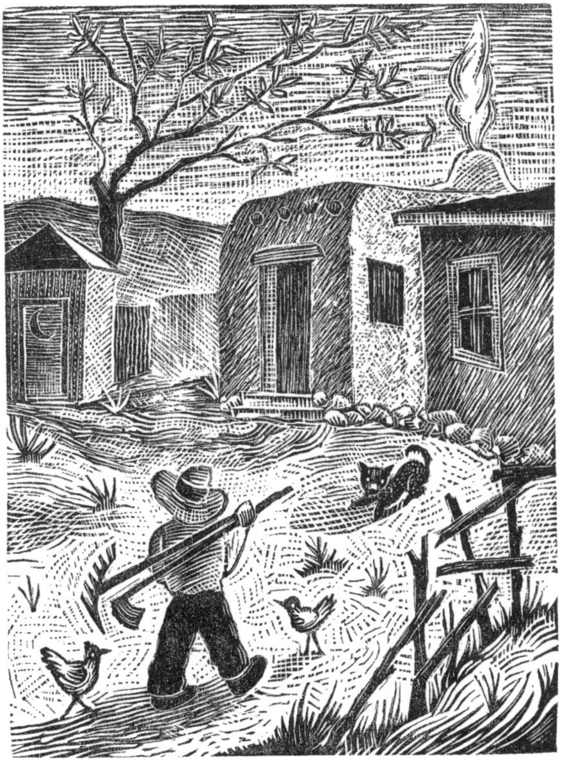

12

INTERIOR OF OLD ADOBE

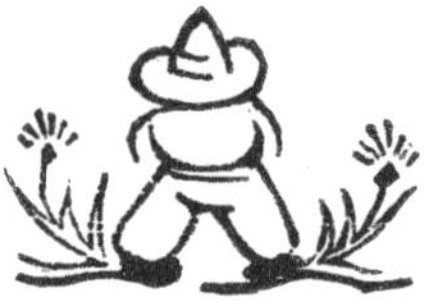

Here we have two little girls that I was to acquire, sitting in front of the corner fireplace burning piñon wood. If you have never been in a small room and had the aroma of piñon you certainly have a treat coming.

This print shows a flagstone floor, but packed dirt was also used, and here again is another treat. They used a little animal blood mixed with our clay-type dirt: the resulting earth floor was one you could sweep, and it was warm for our feet. I think our creator intended for us to live on the earth.

Take notice of the ridge you have to step over to go from room to room: this helps to keep the drafts under control.

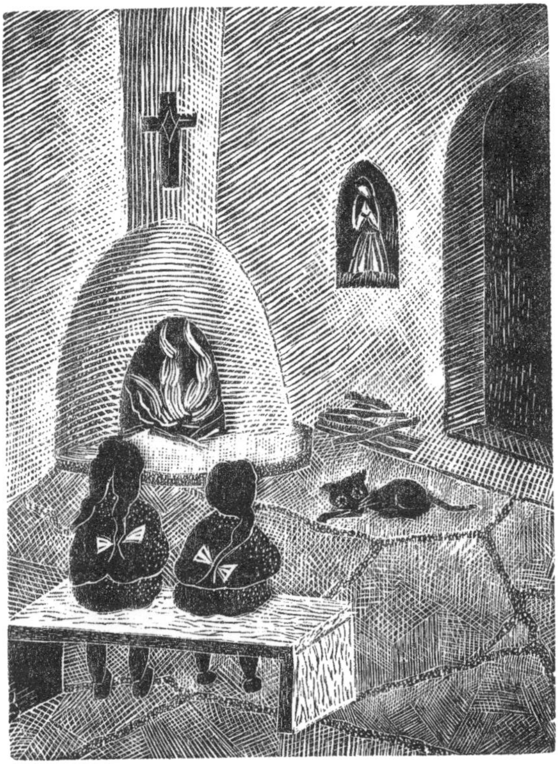

13

INDIAN POTTERY MAKER

An Indian lady and her pots, what could possibly be more compatible than that? After all these years I have never lost my respect for their craftsmanship. They really enjoy and care about the craft they learned from generations past, and time has no place in their effort.

One of these ladies from Tesuque helped my wife in the house for many years. It took a very long time before she was my friend, but it was worth it: she is still a very special lady to me.

We could learn so much from these people if we would only listen.

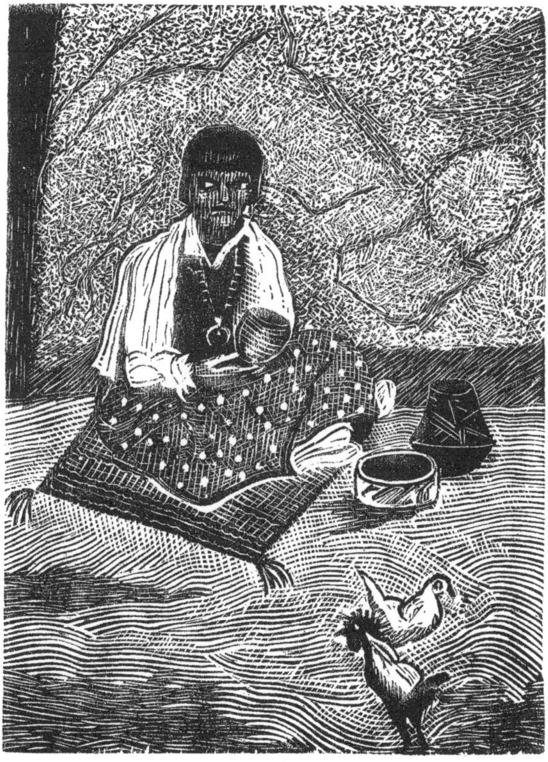

14

SAN ILDEFONSO

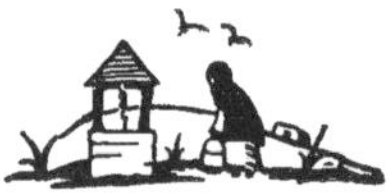

The Black Mesa is in the background, and their Kiva is in the foreground.

The Kiva is where no white person ever treads. The Catholic Spanish priests tried to convert these heathens to their way of thinking and changed the Indian lifestyle very little.

When I visited Santo Domingo I noticed the painted decoration on the front of the church: one time it would be angels and the next time horses, deer, the sun and rain. On inquiring, I was told that when the visiting priest was to arrive, the horses, etc., were painted out and angels took over.

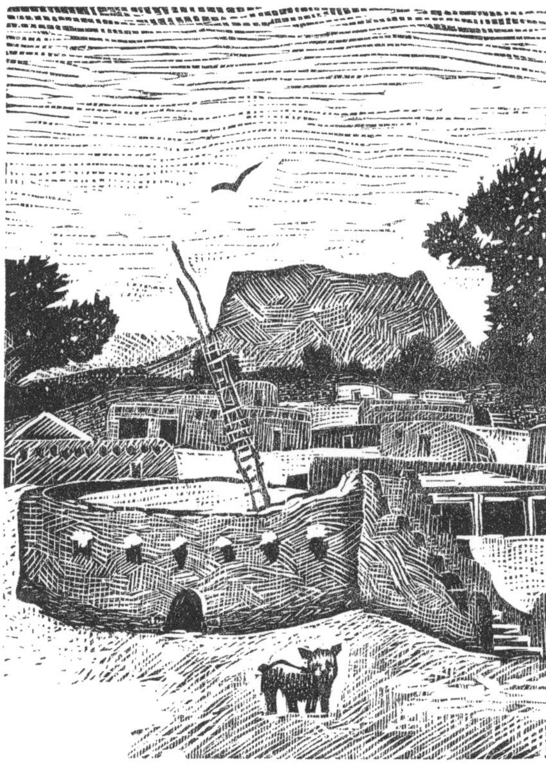

15

CAMEL ROCK

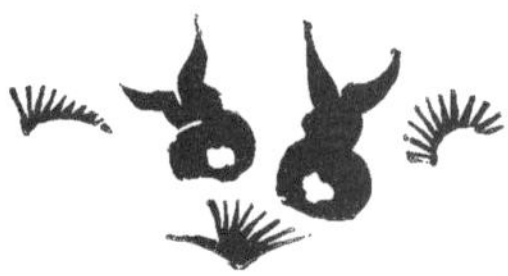

The Creator must have had fun doing this one with simple tools like the wind, rain and time.

In the days of a two-lane dirt road going north, you could stop and climb up to the hump of the camel and maybe see rabbits, doves or maybe a coyote.

Now these are all gone and we have fences, picnic tables, trailers, stores and people.

In checking with Webster, this is called progress. Do we really need it?

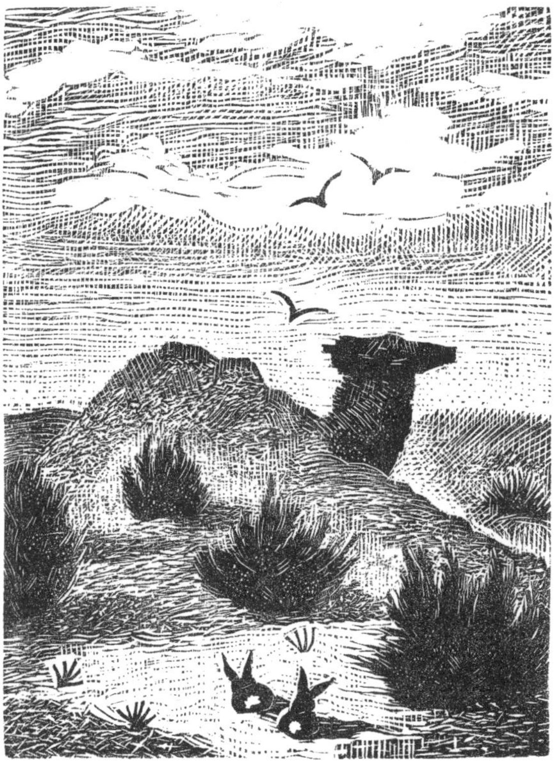

16

SENA PLAZA

Another one of the interesting old buildings —it's important to me, as it was the birthplace of my print shop, a small lever press, where the first very bad woodcut was made.

This building is typical of the old Spanish homes of this period, rectangular with a court or garden in the middle. Before plumbing, the well was usually in the middle of this court. The house often just grew with the family: as the children started new families, more rooms were built.

They learned to be tolerant of each other in trade for security.

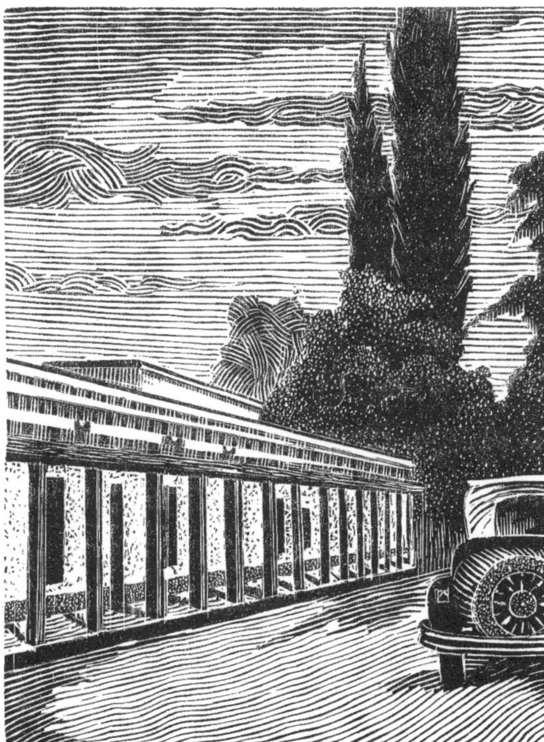

17

MY HOUSE

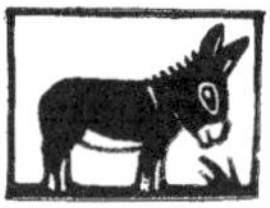

This woodcut print shows the place I built to house the print shop downstairs and a very little apartment upstairs for two little girls, my wife and me.

The outside stairs got us up to an outside porch and our living area. The porch was a good place to entertain a few friends or family, and we also slept out there on beautiful nights. The oversized horno (oven) was for burning the waste paper from the print shop and not for baking bread. The car and the goat were like it was: neighbors were very few, this area was alfalfa fields.

How did we get enough work in a location like this during the depression years? Simple: a good wife with a great personality who liked people. My job was to do the work as well and as quickly and as reasonably as I could. The art work and wood engravings helped.

The incentive was simple, too: the wife and two kids.

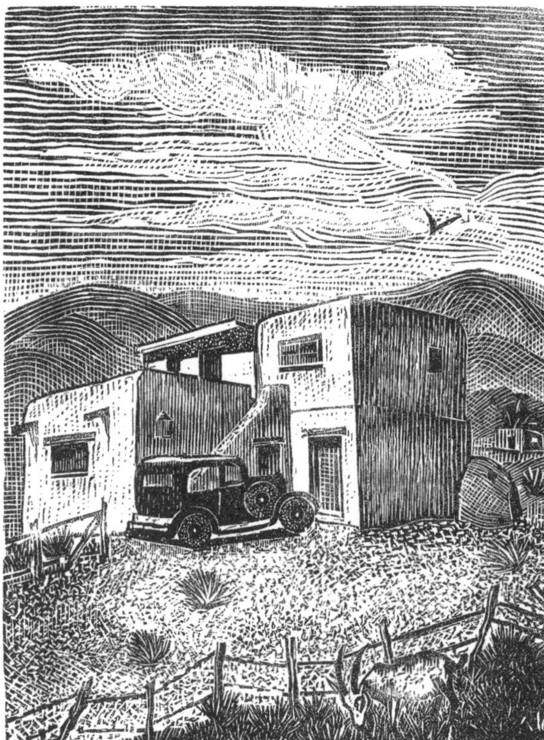

18

BUILDING AN ADOBE

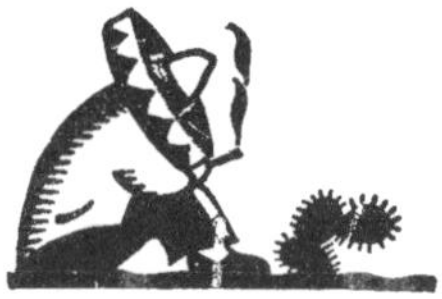

Why build adobe? My reason was simple: no money. Adding a little sand, straw and sun to earth, with the important ingredient of work, we had our adobe bricks. Lumber was very high-priced so we used the minimum. By using large stones in our foundation we saved on cement. No power tools of any kind were used on the original structure— the foundation trench, the mixing of the cement, and making adobes were all done by hand. The door and window frames were made by Sosaya, a carpenter from whom I bought my property.

Adobes are 12″ x 14″ x 4″ and weigh about 25 lbs., so you need a good foundation. They are laid in mud mortar, three rows at a time, and allowed to settle at least 3 or 4 days. Patience is another ingredient necessary in Santa Fe.

There was no architect or contractor, just a stupid young man who needed a house badly for the family and shop.

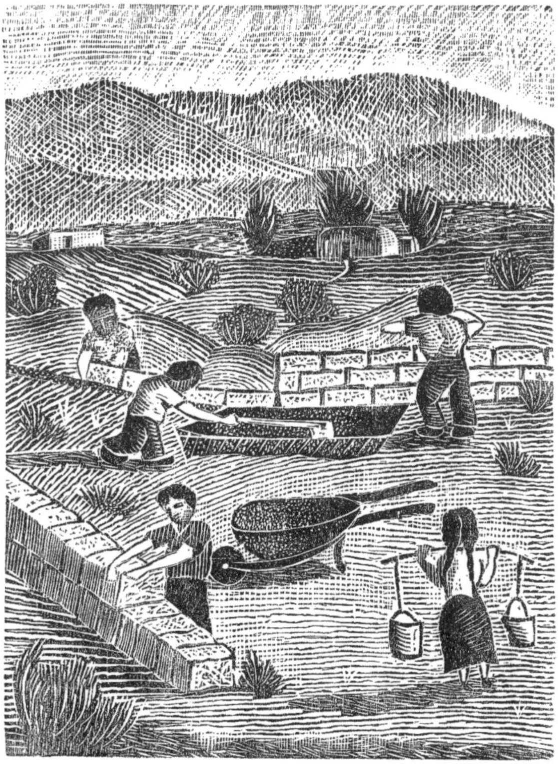

19

I WENT FISHING

Probably did this too much! I was able to get up early, run up to the Pecos and fish a couple of hours and not see another human being before the print shop had to open. In the evenings I was able to do the same thing. To have a beautiful day surrounded by peace with the only sounds coming from the clear mountain stream that would safely quench your thirst, and the excitement of a trout jumping at your dry fly—you just cannot worry about how you are going to do that printing job.

These simple things replaced going to the theater and art galleries.

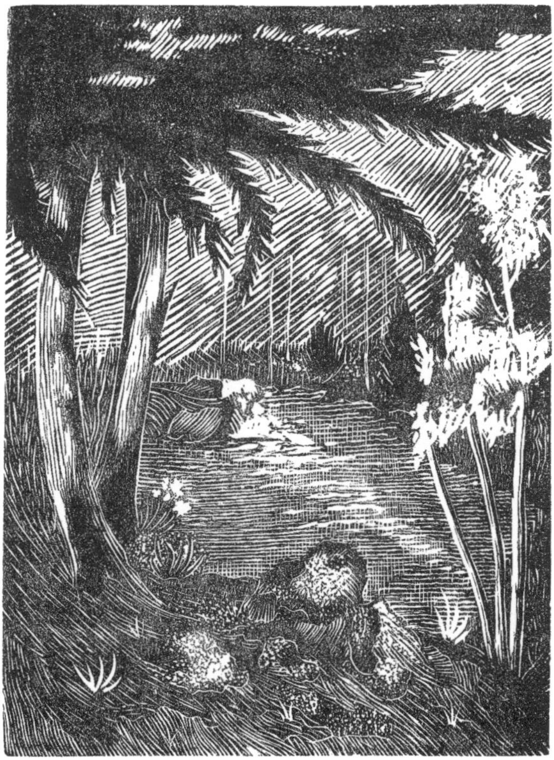

20

McCROSSEN WEAVERS

These people were important to me as one of my first customers for printing who were to last for many years.

Like myself, they started small and grew steadily, using hand-operated looms, making some of the finest materials I have ever seen. Neckties became one of their main mail-order products. Weaving fits this area and the people well: it is a natural trade. So when McCrossen's grew, they did not have trouble getting help.

This print is of their first location, an old abandoned church on lower San Francisco Street.

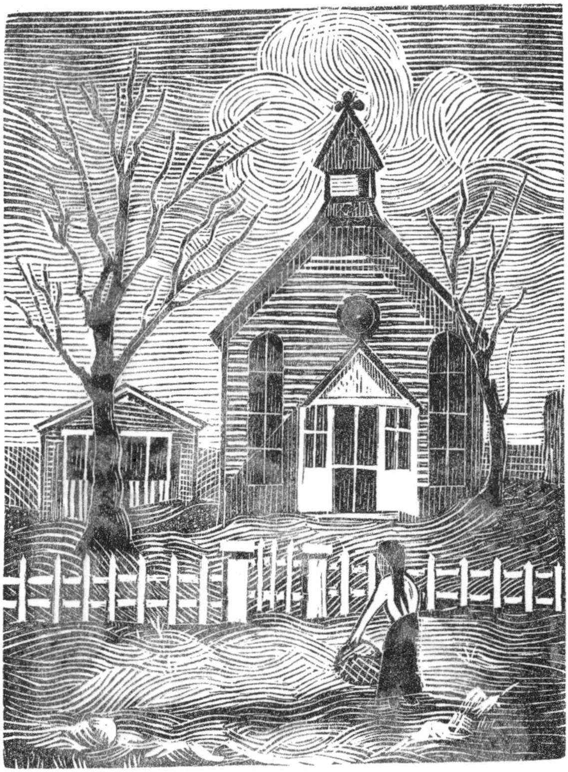

21

SATURDAY NIGHT

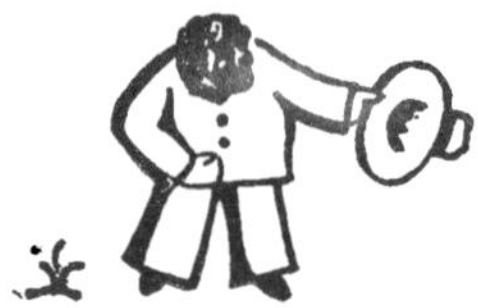

The shop is closed, the moon is full, the dogs are howling, a good old friend drops by with a little home brew for relaxing. These are prohibition days, and that was all we had. It was bad but it didn't take long before we were really relaxed! At the time, it seemed the thing to do, get the guitar and join the dogs. This, like the home brew, was very bad, but when you are relaxed you do not notice.

Now it is much simpler: a couch, a can of beer, t.v. and a ball game. But there is just one difference: your good friend is not there.

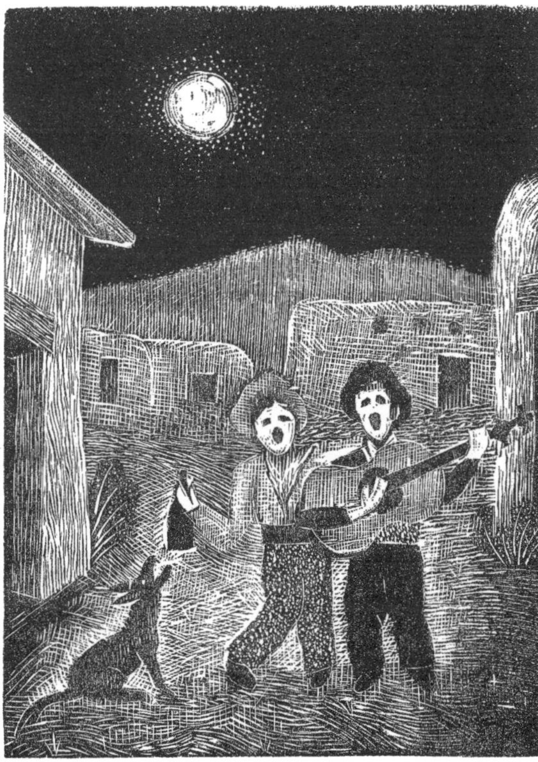

22

LAMY CHAPEL AND BISHOPS LODGE

Bishop Lamy built the little chapel north of Santa Fe, and lived in it while they were rebuilding the Cathedral. He also had an orchard.

Mr. and Mrs. Thorpe bought and built a guest ranch there. Mr. Thorpe did not get to enjoy it very long, but Mrs. Thorpe ran it for many years and built it into a prosperous venture with excellent taste. She maintained the chapel and many visitors have enjoyed it.

They were also very good customers for the print shop as well as friends to my wife and me.

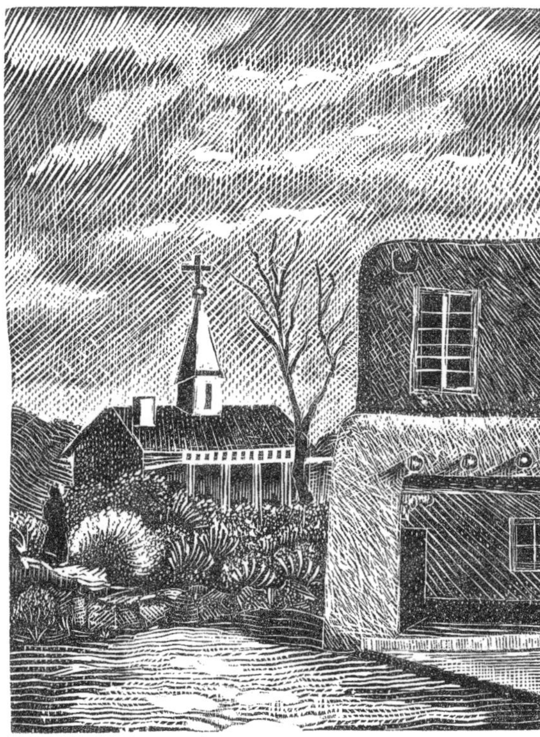

OLD MILL ON ACEQUIA MADRE

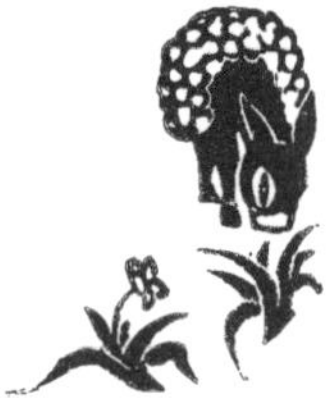

This old house was owned by Pem and Irving Parsons when I first saw it. In the basement was an old grinding stone run by a water wheel off the irrigation ditch.

At one time, the mill served this area of small farms.

It stayed much the same for many years, until Pem died and the house was sold. Now, after being remodeled two or three times, it is a pretentious million-dollar home and the grinding stone is part of a fountain in the garden.

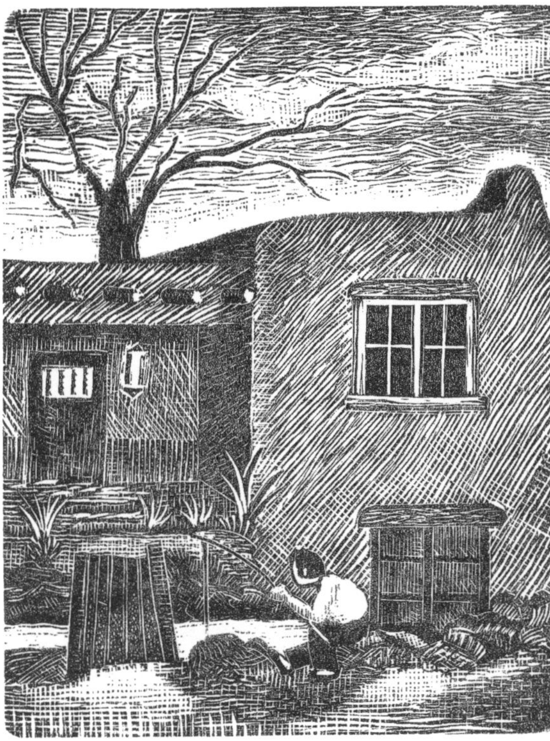

24

WENT DUCK HUNTING

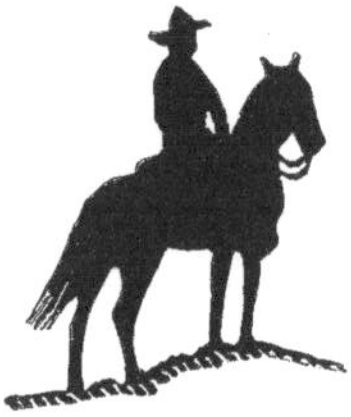

The memories of these events are what sustain me now: the companionship with my brothers-in-law and friends, the outdoors, and the laughter mostly at ourselves.

Our wives wished we would grow up and not act like boys, but decided we could have been doing something much more harmful.

We all tried to get them to pick and clean our game like the pioneer women. No way!

Occasionally we got together and had a game dinner—quail, ducks, doves, maybe even a goose.

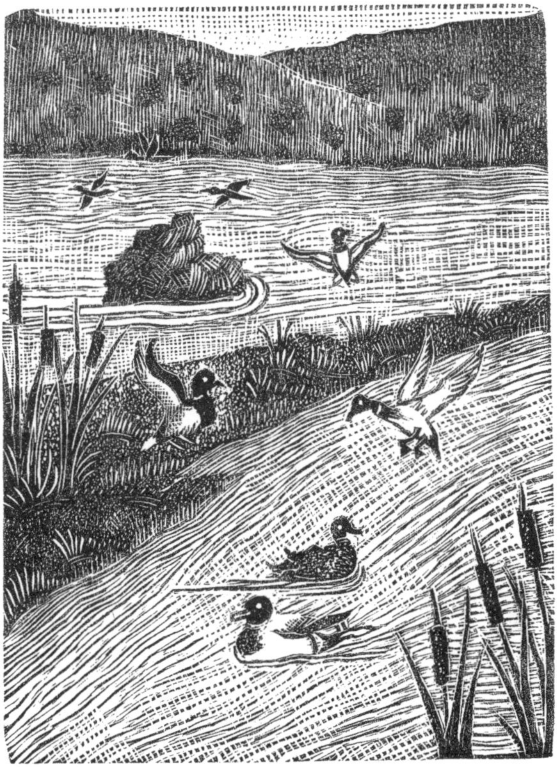

25

SANTUARIO

If you were to drive north of Santa Fe on one of the dirt roads of that time, you would see groups of adobe buildings which blended into the rolling piñon-covered hills. And if there was a church, you could assume there was a village.

The only way the people could get a church was for them all to get together and build it; and because it was a house for their God it was bigger and better than the other buildings. Then they needed an altar, candlesticks, benches, saints; and once again the only way these farmers and their wives had was to build with the materials they had—cottonwood and pine, old gasoline and coal oil tins, simple hand tools. I think you would be impressed as I was with what these untrained craftsmen accomplished.

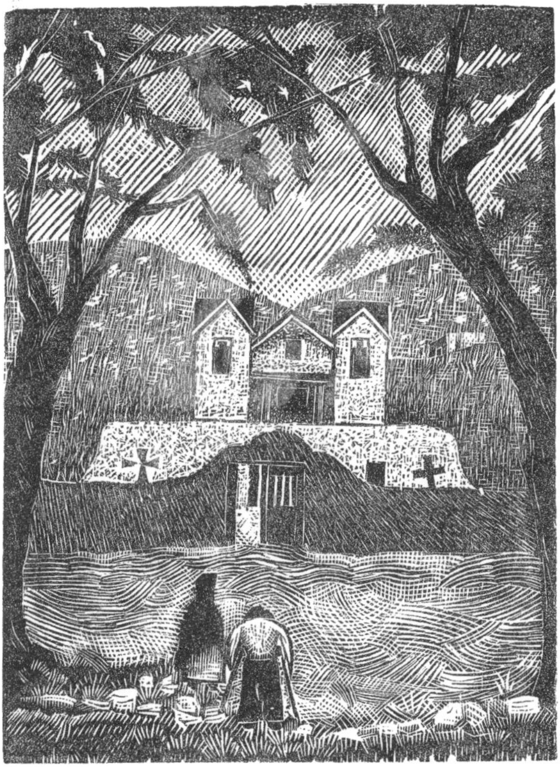

26

WEAVERS IN CHIMAYO

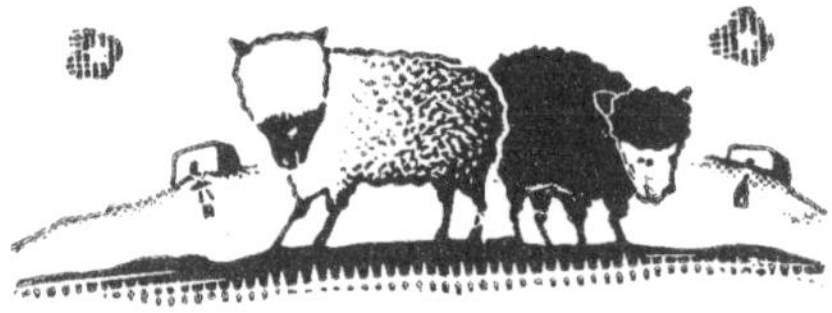

All these villages seem to have their own specialty: Chimayo became famous for their blankets, Truchas for carving cottonwood, Pojoaque for bootleg whiskey.

We have two of the old Chimayo large blankets which we took in trade for printing in the early 30s. The wool seems to be handspun, the colors natural dye, the design simple, and the result beautiful.

Now there is commercial yarn, more uniform and less texture; the colors are much brighter and varied; and the designs are much more complicated. But the craftsmanship is very good and sometimes also beautiful in a different way.

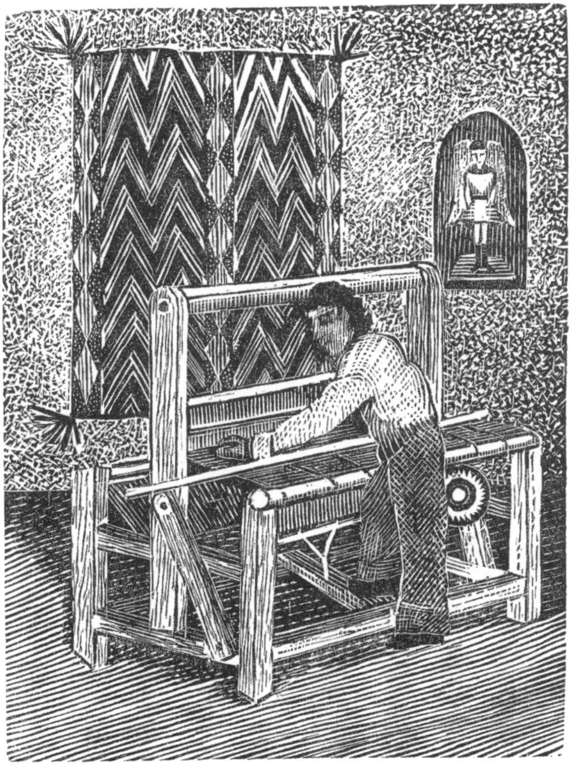

27

FUNERAL PROCESSION

Here is one of my favorite memories. It was up in the Truchas area. We were able from a little distance to watch a funeral procession. Usually the pallbearers carry the coffin, but this time they used a wagon—maybe the deceased was an influential member of the community?

A simple homemade box: as usual it was a nice day and they did not want to close the lid sooner than necessary.

I wish to be convinced why this simplicity is no longer acceptable in our culture.

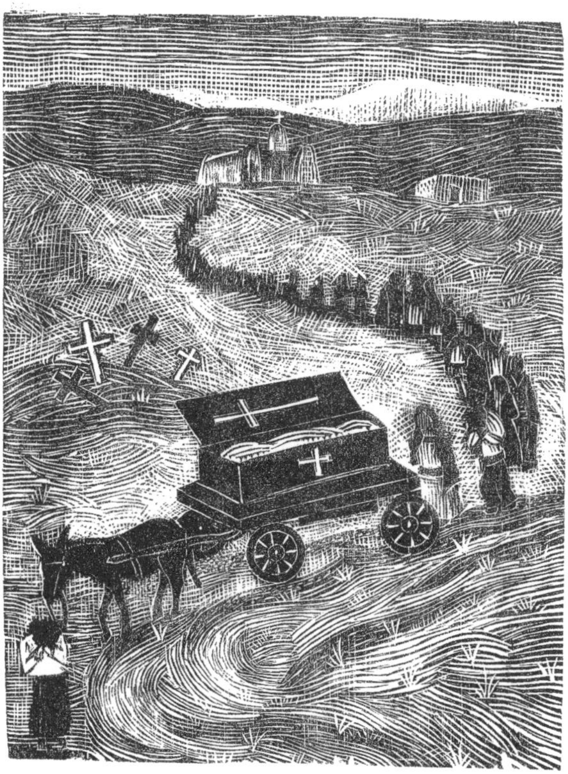

28

GORMLEY'S GENERAL STORE

A neighborhood general store just a little walk from our home, they had everything we needed: groceries, sewing material, paint for upkeep of the house, alfalfa or chicken feed for the livestock. They met you with a "Hi, Willard, how are the kids and wife and all of the rest of the family, and tell me about anybody in the area who is having trouble."

My very little girls would walk over from our house to buy a little candy and we did not worry: hard to believe now.

The Gormleys probably sold and shipped out more piñon nuts than anyone in 1916—25 tons!

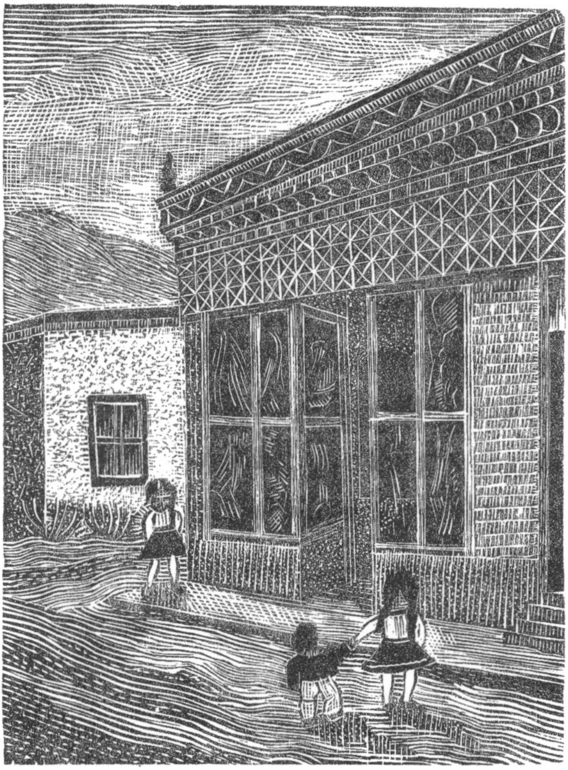

29

MYERS' HOME

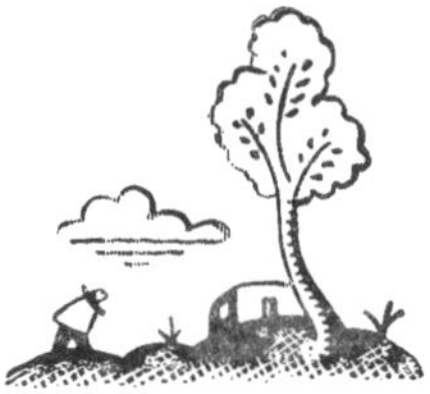

Mr. and Mrs. Datus Myers were important people in this period of my life. He was one of the best painters of this area and time. They built this most beautiful home on Camino del Monte Sol, the same street on which the Cinco Pintores had built theirs.

This house with the thick adobe walls and natural flowing lines, with an interior of heavy Spanish oak furniture, had a studio for Datus with a huge north window. There was a beautiful parquet floor for Eve, their daughter, who developed into a professional dancer.

Many very rewarding hours were spent in this house.

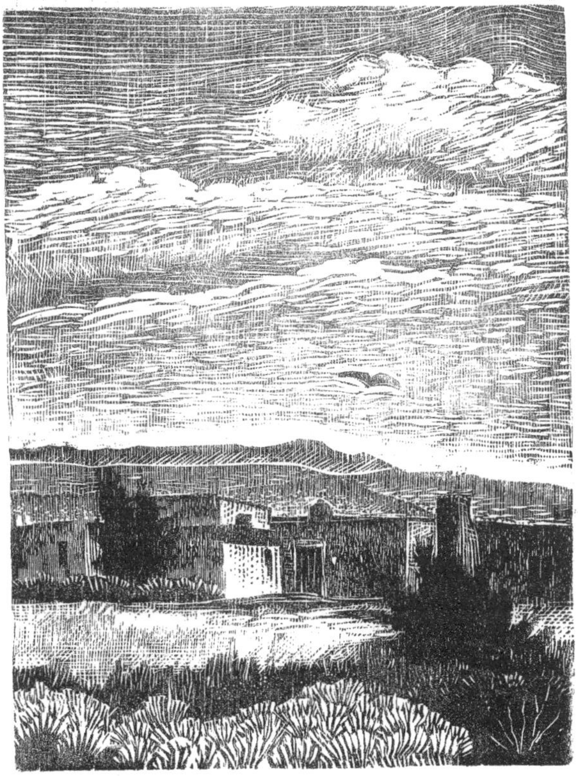

SANTO

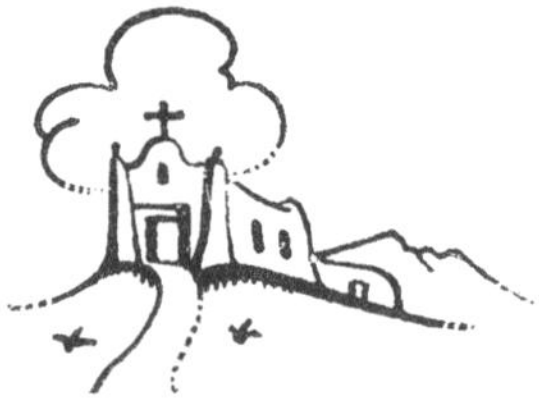

Religion is such an important part of the Catholic people of this area, and if you are to know and understand them you must try to understand their faith.

Some of their best creative work is done in their carvings and paintings of the Santos, Retablos, Cristos, and Madonnas, especially when they are done for their local church or for their own home altars. When they get involved in selling them to the tourists and start making many alike, they lose interest and the main ingredient is gone.

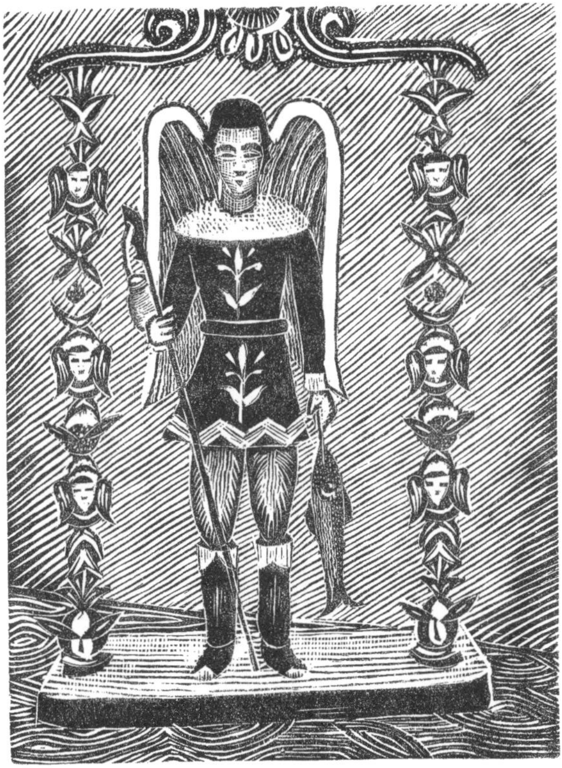

OLD CROSS OF THE MARTYRS

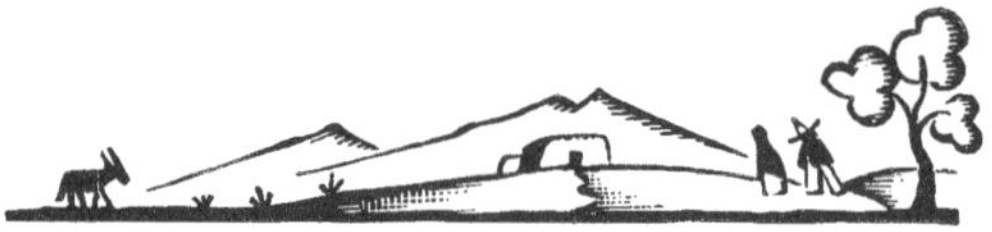

The Pueblo Indians were the first people of the area with their own culture and faith, trying to make a living farming this arid land with occasional raids from the Navajos and Apaches who did not seem to like the idea of that kind of work.

Then came the Spaniards with greed for gold and the need to convert all other people to their faith and way of living. These conquerors were not kind to those that resisted. So the Northern Pueblos got together and escorted them off their land. The Indians did not try to convert them: just go home and leave us alone.

Even to this day they do not get along very well.

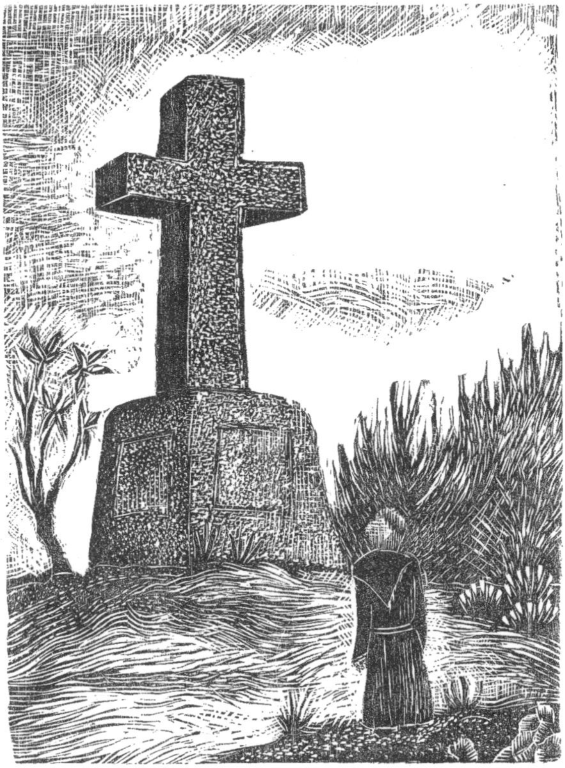

32

WEDDING

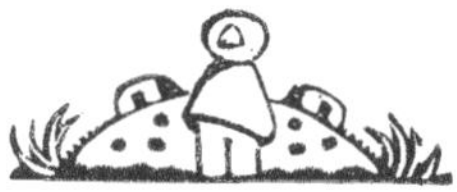

Now we have a very happy occasion with Mass at the church so the knot is tied very tightly to hold up until death do they part. The cars are decorated with lots of flowers and they ride around the plaza honking their horns and waving to all with much laughter.

Maybe all of this does help because they seem to stay together above the average.

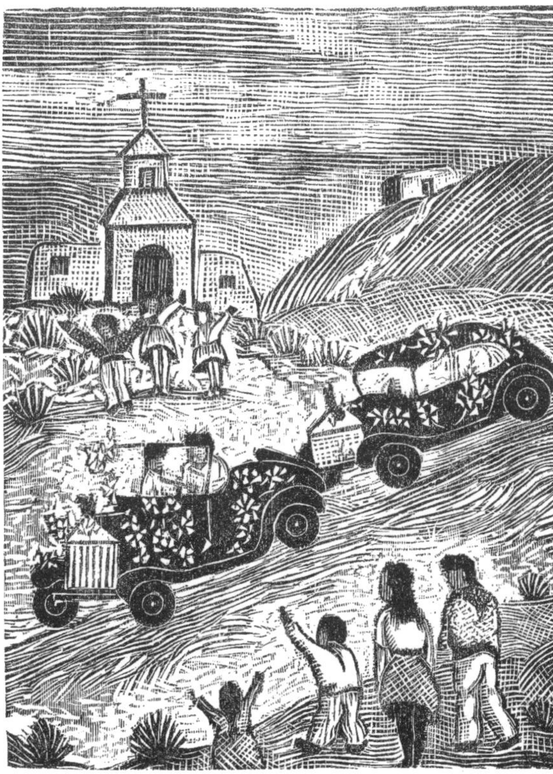

33

FLIRTING IN THE PLAZA

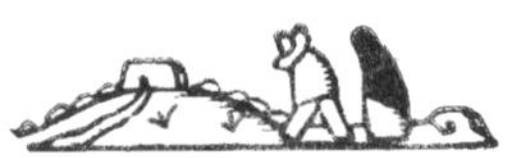

Here we have more fun: the boys walking around the plaza one way and the girls walking the other, each trying to attract the other. It was fun to sit on a bench with your kids and watch them.

After all, when it is death do you part, it takes a lot of looking to make it worthwhile.

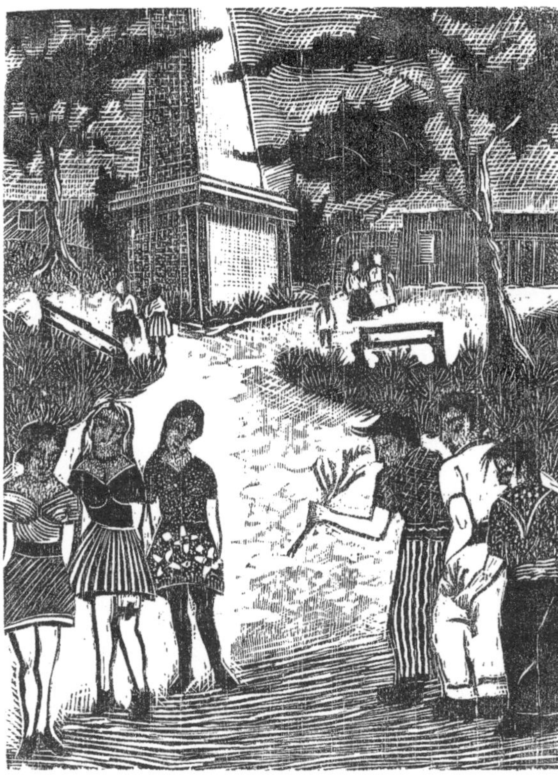

34

MISS CHRISTMAS

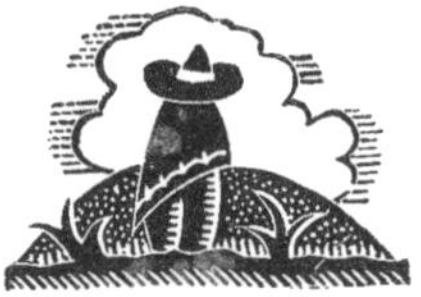

In one of the pleasant traditions which I have never seen before, the children on Christmas eve would come by and knock on the door and when opened call out, "Miss Christmas!" You would invite them in and they would entertain you with a little poem, song, dance, or maybe just a big smile. And in return you would offer them candy, cookies or whatever.

This tradition terminated in the thirties, if my memory is working.

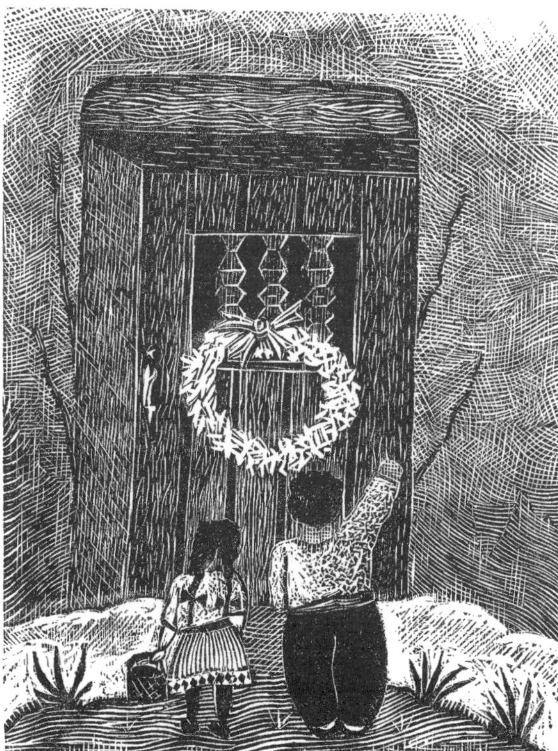

35

FAROLITOS

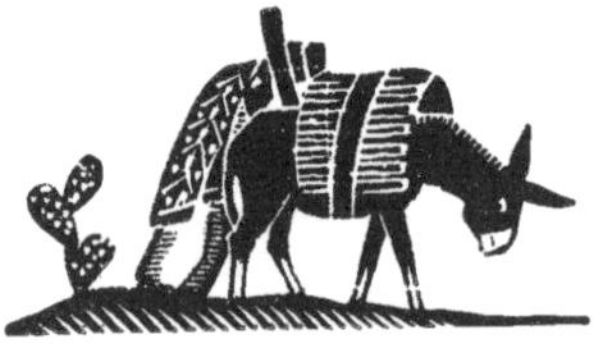

Another very decorative tradition, and so simple: a paper sack, an inexpensive white candle and sand. They give off a soft light and last a long time.

You used to outline the different elevations of your house, or help your guest along the path of your garden, or just a few to let them know this is where the party is.

One of the most interesting examples was La Fonda Hotel.

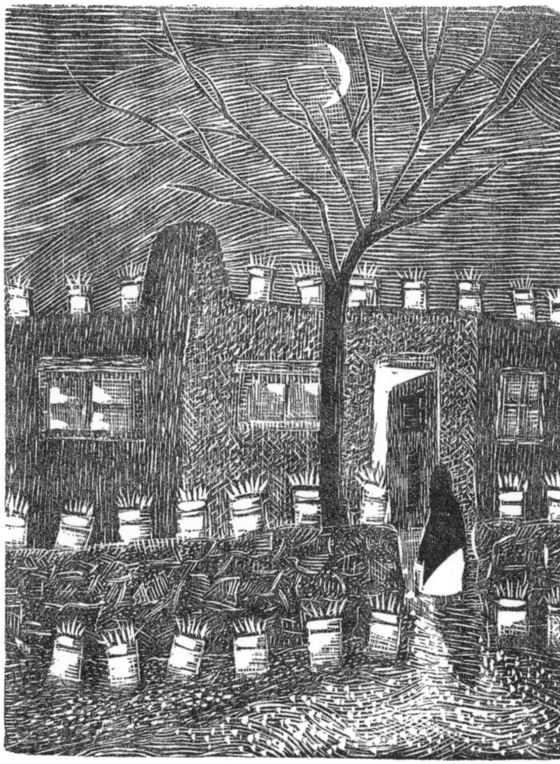

36

PROCESSION TO THE CROSS OF THE MARTYRS

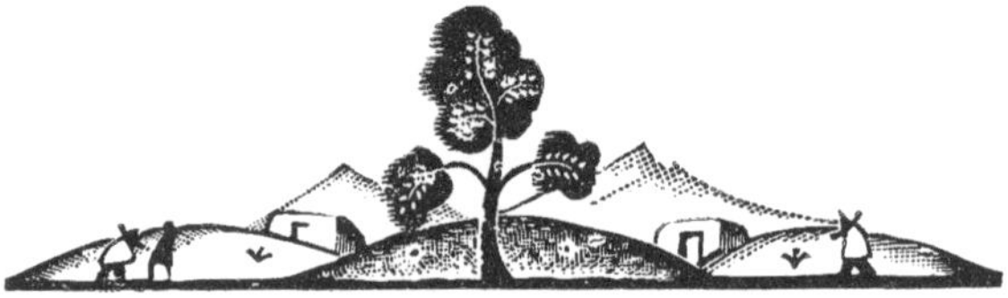

This print is my impression of the procession to the Cross of the Martyrs during Fiesta by the Spanish people in memory of the priests who died during the Indian revolt. It started at the Cathedral and ended at the Cross. They all carried candles and the path was illuminated with little bonfires.

Fiesta was a combination of religion and merriment: you went to church, then you sang and danced in the plaza. If you were hungry, there was the best chile in the world—homemade by the Spanish women.

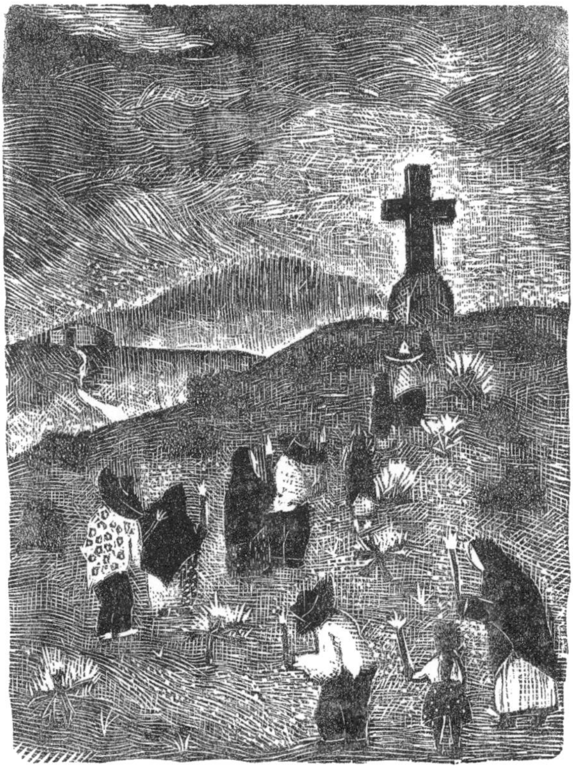

37

PROCESSION TO THE SANTUARIO

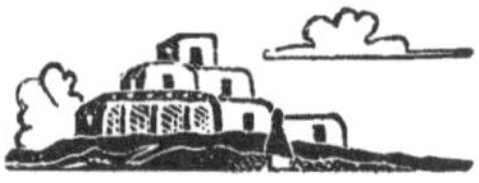

This is not much different from sanctuaries all over the world. In this case, there seems to be a miraculous effect in the earth inside the church, causing quite a hole from samples taken; and there are the usual crutches that were no longer needed.

The pilgrimage at Easter has become much larger and more social than it was in the thirties.

That little guy in the wagon doesn't count—you must walk, and if you carry a heavy cross that helps. Some walk for many miles.

The crosses on the side of the road I have been told are placed there where the Penitentes stop to rest when carrying their dead.

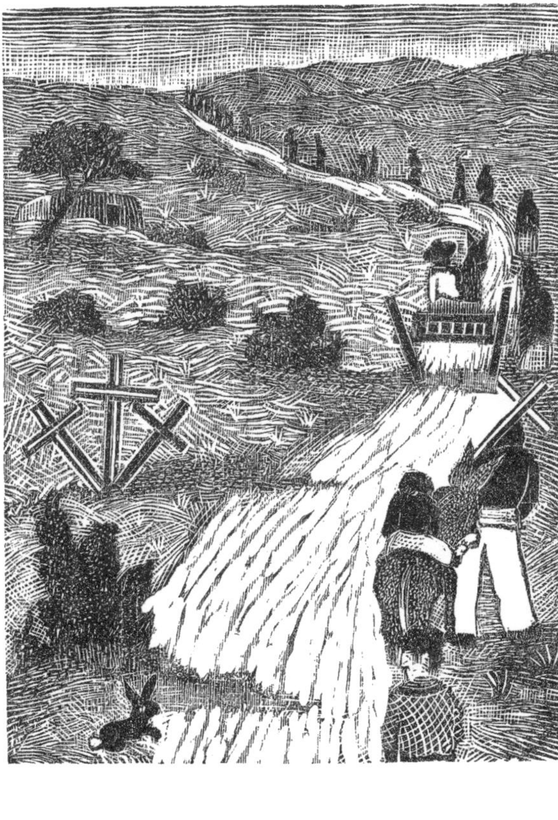

38

CHILE PEPPERS OUT TO DRY

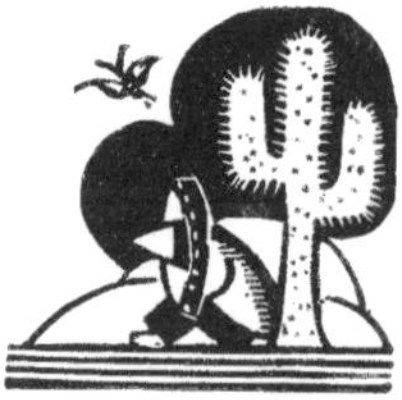

In the fall, the chile peppers are gathered and tied in long strands or ristras and hung over the edge of the flat roofs to dry. They turn a bright red: you look over a little village with all the homes drying chile! Please let your imagination complete this print.

When dry, you hang a ristra near the kitchen for the most addictive dinners I know of.

This northern area is famous for their chile.

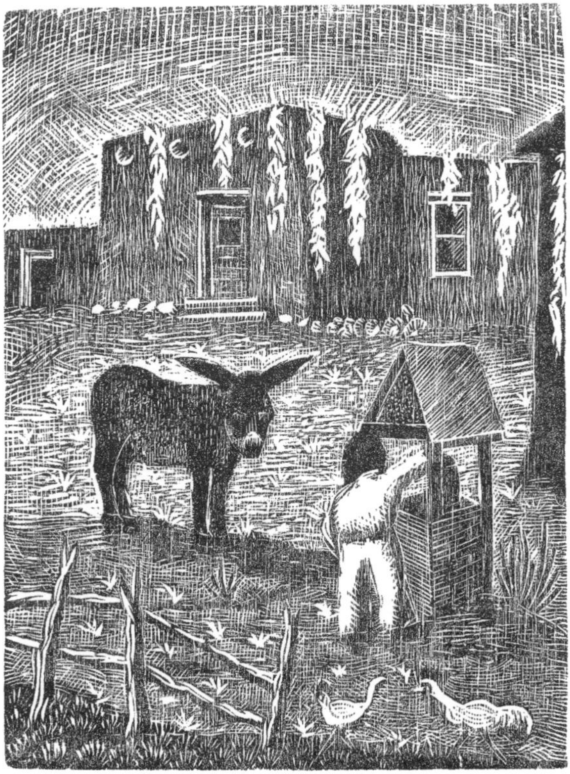

39

INDIAN LADY BAKING BREAD

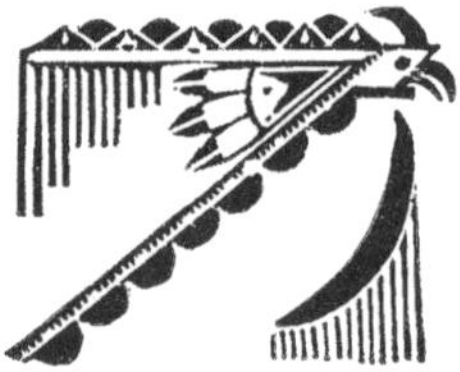

There is not much to say about an Indian lady baking bread: it is done by ladies all over the world. It is a fact, however, that she built her own oven outside, and her round thick loaves have more substance and taste than the white bread at the supermarket.

And the fact that she herself is so colorful and interesting adds to it. If she forgets to cover the opening of the oven when she finishes her baking, the dogs find it makes a great dog house.

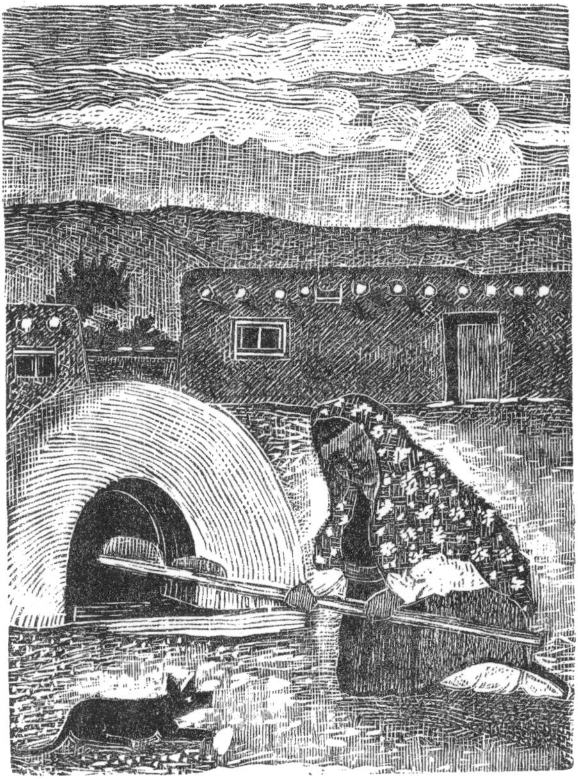

40

MY LITTLE SHRINE

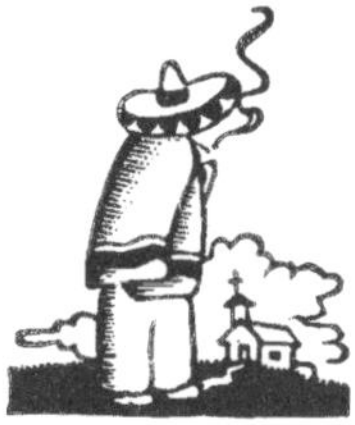

Thanks to my good wife who was a knowledgeable gardener we had a pleasant garden surrounded by fences to keep the animals out. We decided a wall would give us a little more privacy and cut down on the wind.

As usual, it also created a problem. Our neighbor across the lane was a widow living alone. We were fond of her and she had enjoyed looking at our garden from her porch.

When I built the wall, this shrine was made for her. The children up the lane seemed to enjoy it also and kept bringing flowers for the little Madonna.

One evening when I came home, two little girls were kneeling—certainly much more than I deserved.

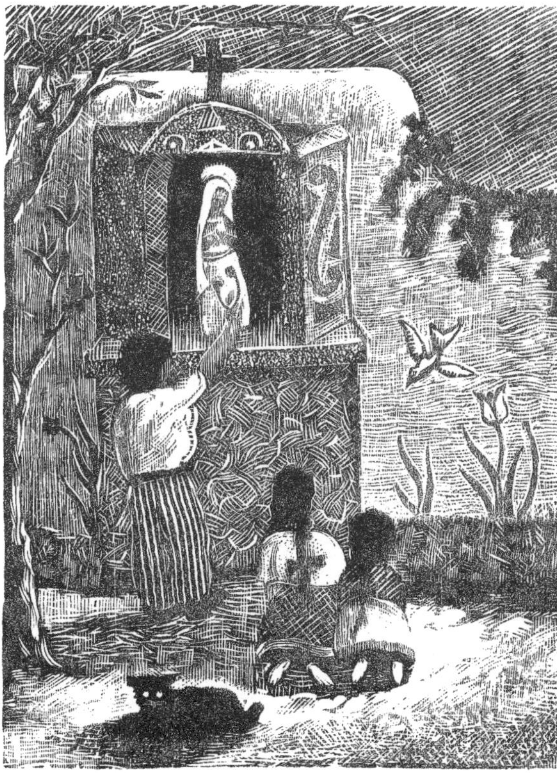

41

CHAPEL IN GLORIETA

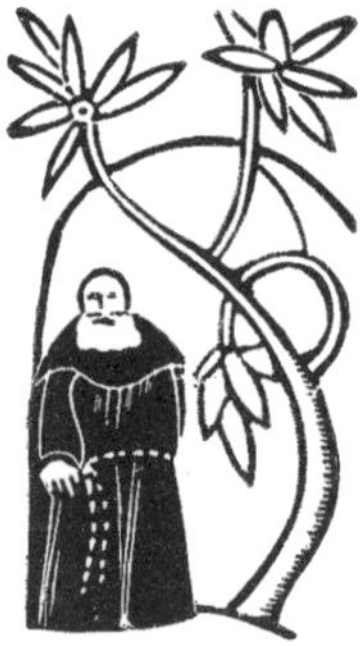

This chapel was on the way to the Pecos River where much time was spent fishing and once in a while painting. The chapel impressed me because it was always so well kept, and the white chickens seemed part of it.

In those days, traveling priests would come a few times a year to take care of the villagers, say Mass, hear confession, bless the dead, baptize the babies, and also marry the babies' mothers and dads.

It seems like women's lib and living together are not quite as new as you may think.

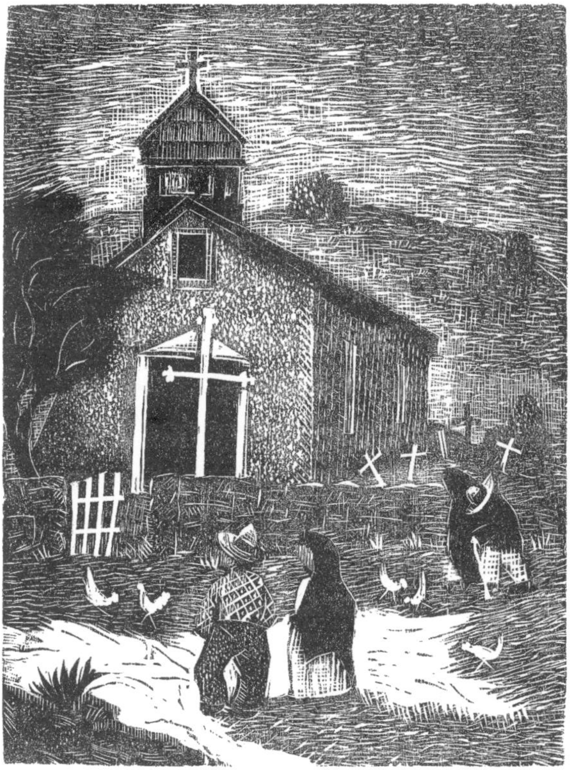

42

SANTA FE FIESTA

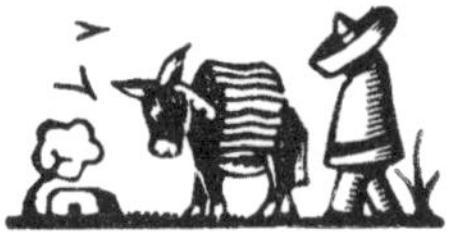

Held in the fall much the same as fiestas all over the world, there were two or three days to visit with friends and hoop it up a little with dancing, song and wine, besides the religious processions and fun parades for the children.

In the thirties, old man gloom was introduced by artist Will Shuster to help us put behind our troubles and start the merriment by burning him.

Religion and history played an important part in the celebration that was managed by the people and for the people of Santa Fe.

Now it is difficult to remember what it was like.

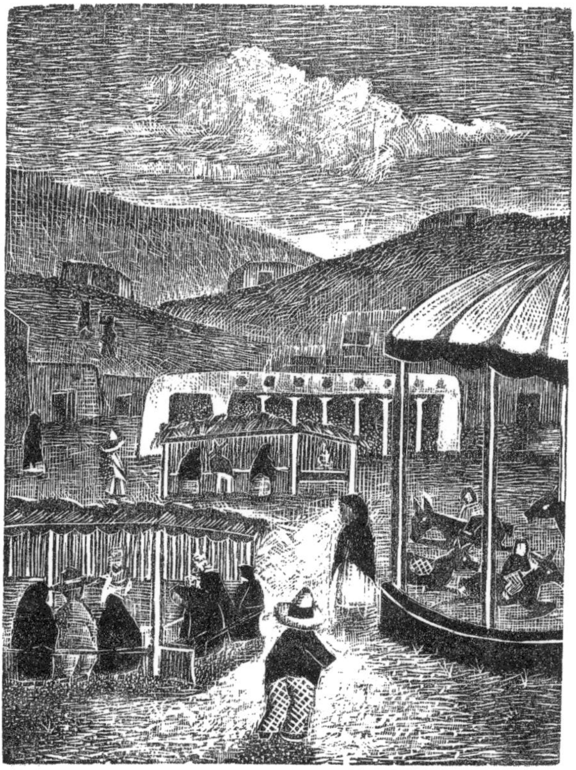

43

INDIAN WOMEN PLASTERING

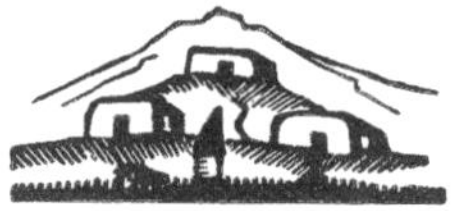

During one of my visits to one of the Indian pueblos, I noticed Indian women plastering the church with only their hands while the Indian men watched with admiration. It seems they also build the corner fireplaces and the hornos to bake their bread.

Returning home, I asked my wife to take a little ride to show her how the Indian women occupied themselves. Bertha informed me she did not have any Indian blood, and graphically indicated what she thought of my ideas! Oh well, it was worth a try.

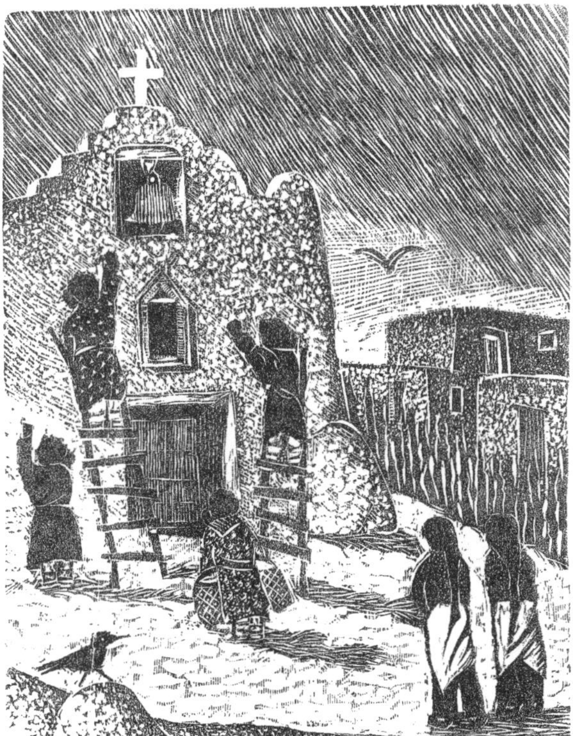

44

CAR STUCK IN SAND

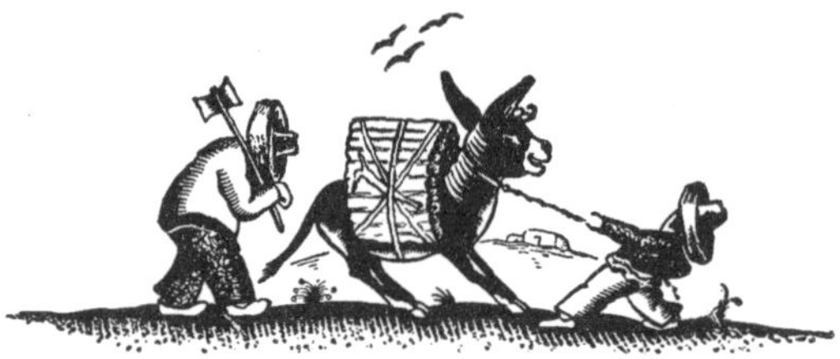

This country was all open range—no fences—and the only paving was between Bernalillo and Albuquerque. It was our drag strip, probably went 35 or 40 miles an hour.

Since the open range was often as good or better than the roads and more fun, we would cut across country; fixing and changing tires and getting unstuck seemed part of life.

Then came better roads and fences to keep the livestock in and us out. It is certainly more comfortable, so what is my trouble not thinking it is better?

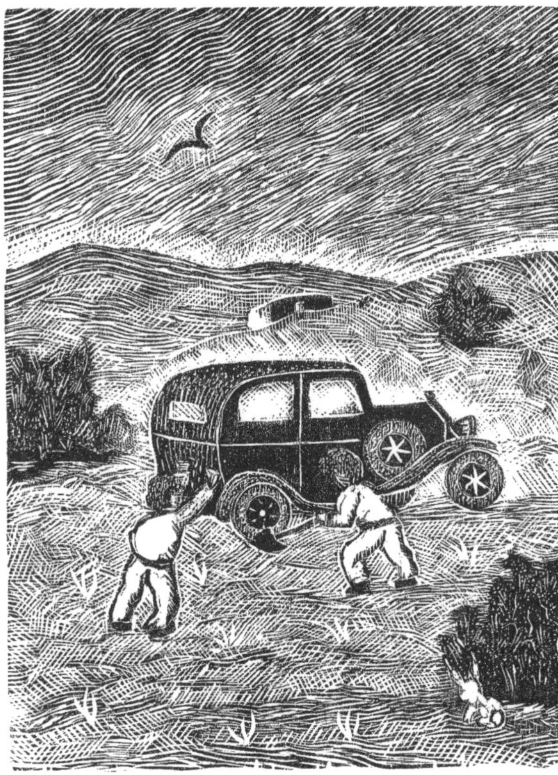

45

SOSAYA LANE

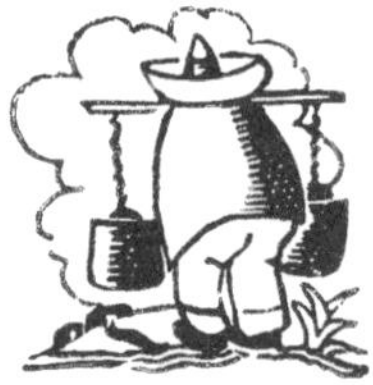

Here we are looking north down Sosaya Lane from our house to the home my brother-in-law had built just before we built ours.

There are my two little girls with their little very black dog who sure did not have any papers. They are on their way to Gormley's General Store for their ration of lollipops. This was about a two city block walk down Acequia Madre and Gormley Lane.

It is very sad to know we would not dare to let them do this today.

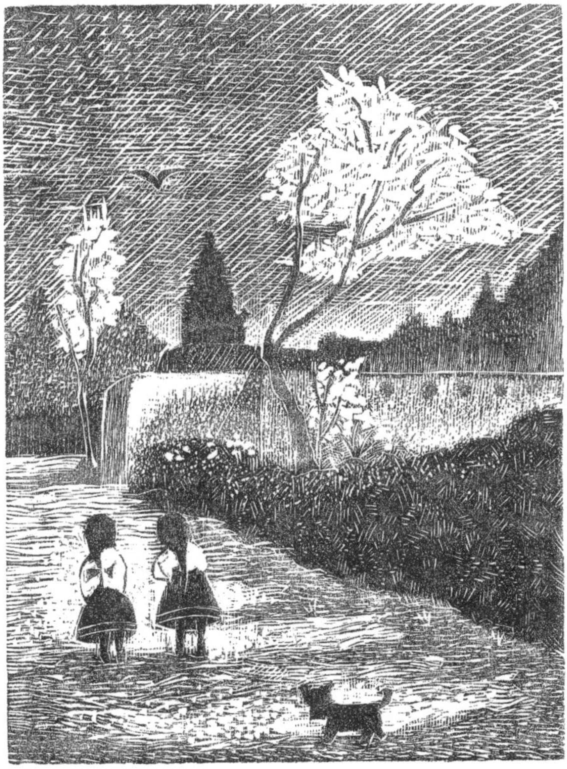

46

405 SOSAYA LANE

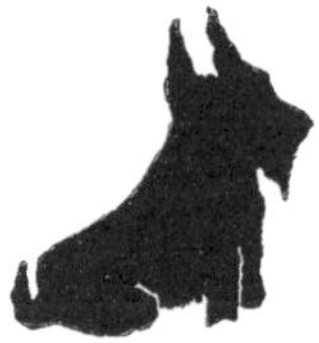

This is the front of our home and print shop as it looked in 1943, and the outside looks much the same today. When the print shop was sold, the inside was converted into our home. What was the composing room and bindery turned into our living room. What was the press room turned into our kitchen and dining area. An inside staircase was built and upstairs were bedrooms. Bertha's office and showroom is where I now do my work.

It is now time to get back to reality. Thank you for the visit.

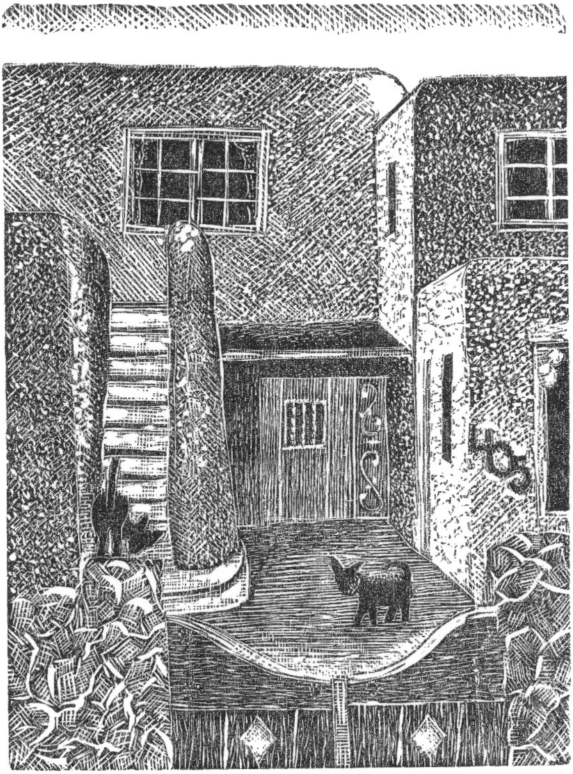

I WISH TO THANK

My family and friends for the push, when my self-starter was not working; Rick for keeping me with the text—I sure needed that.

This edition printed offset lithography by P. Chan & Edward (HK)
Set in Arrighi
Woodcut in maple
Paper: 148 gsm Mohawk Superfine
Copyright by Willard F. Clark

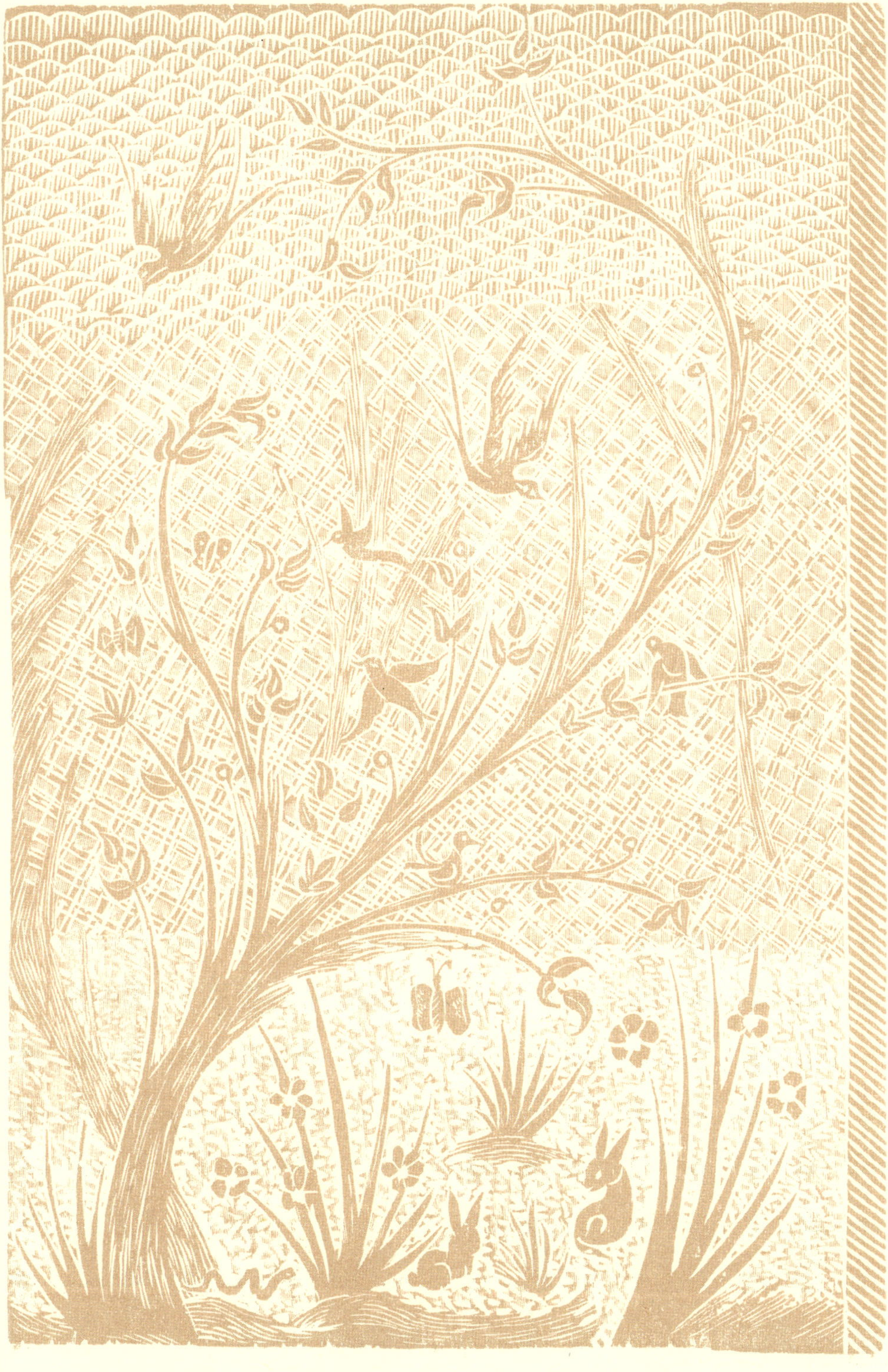

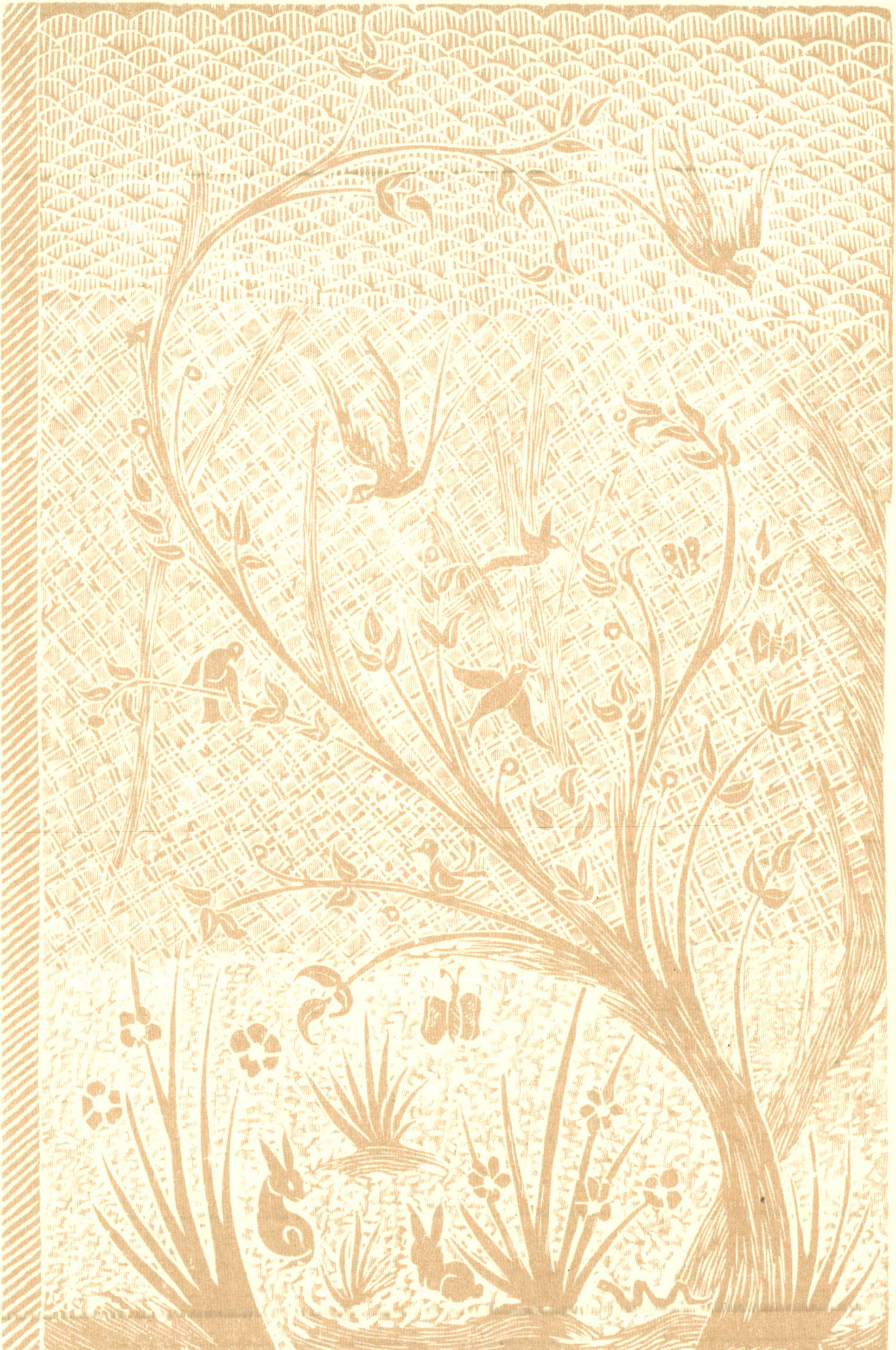

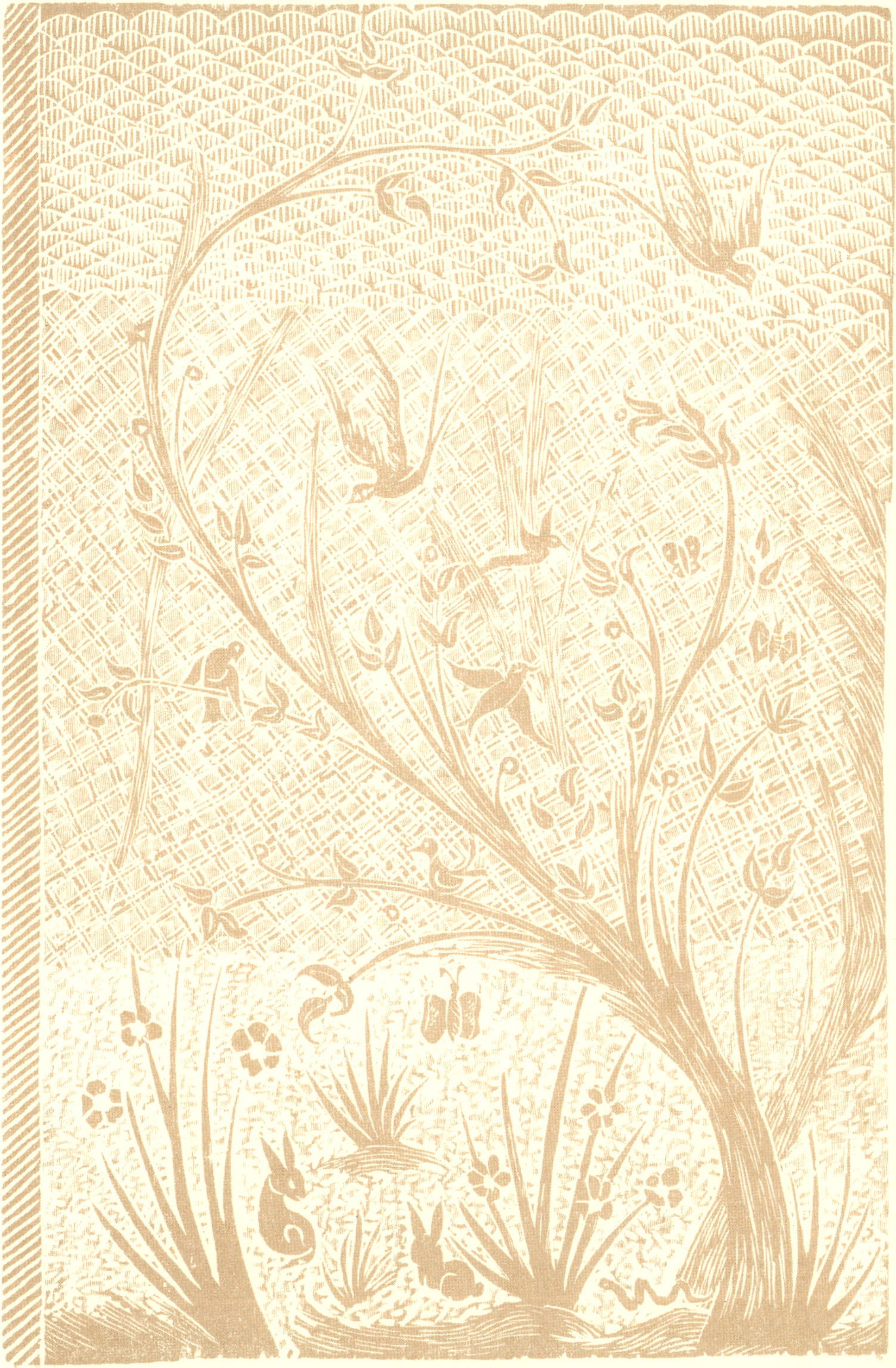

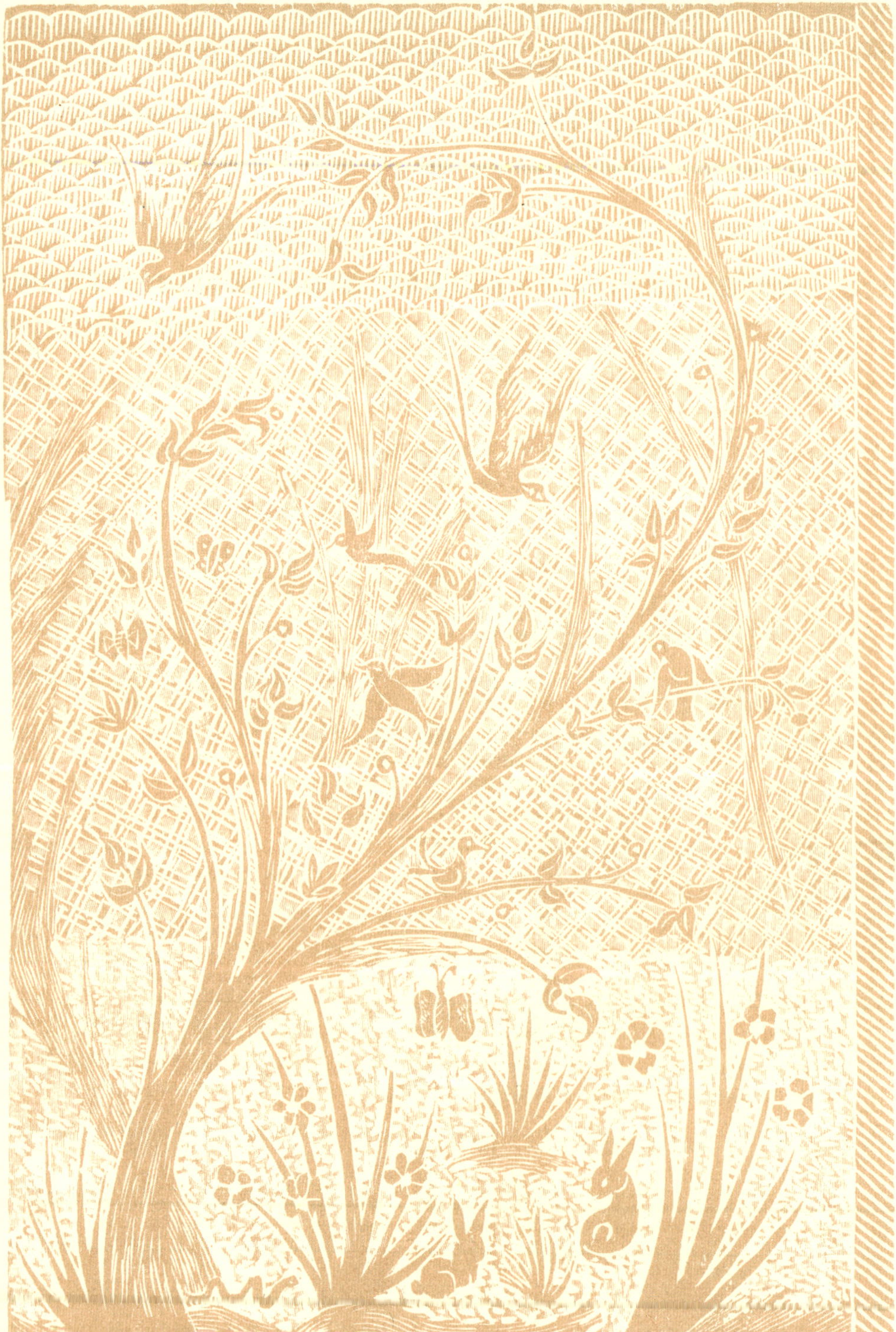